MY BUCKET
OF
SAND

**Other Books Authored
or Edited by
Sheila Jones**

9 to 5 and Spiritually Alive

To Live Is Christ: An Interactive Study of Philippians
co-authored with Thomas A. Jones

Life and Godliness for Everywoman:
A Handbook for Joyful Living (Vol 1)

Life and Godliness for Everywoman:
A Handbook for Joyful Living (Vol 2)

The Fine Art of Hospitality
co-edited with Betty Dyson

Finding Balance

MY BUCKET

OF

SAND

And Other Spiritual Thoughts

Volume Two
Wisdom for Life Series

Sheila Jones

www.dpibooks.org

My Bucket of Sand
©2009 by DPI Books
5016 Spedale Court #331
Spring Hill, TN 37174

Printed in the United States of America

Cover Design: Brian Branch
Cover Photo: fotosearch
Interior Design: Thais Gloor

ISBN: 978-1-57782-237-0

To my three precious daughters

Amy
Bethany
Corrie

You are my treasures.

I love you.

Contents

Wisdom for Life 9
1. My Bucket of Sand 11
2. Connecting the Dots 14
3. God, Don't Drop Me 18
4. From One Goose to Another.......................................21
5. Special Gifts: A Hug and a Kiss.................................23
6. Freedom in Christ..25
7. Don't Freeze-Frame...27
8. Canned or Fresh 29
9. Do Not Be Anxious 33
10. Keep on Walking 38
11. Carried Along 44
12. The Gift of Laughter 47
13. Lift the Other Foot 52
14. The Wilma Vitamin...54
15. God-Breathed 58
16. Getting Rid of Darkness 60
17. I Don't Need Any Help 63
18. Joy on the Journey 66
19. For Their Sake 71
20. Ever Feel Trapped? 74
21. Do Not Worry..76
22. Be Sympathetic 80
23. No Fishing Allowed 83

24. Keep the Welcome Mat Out 86
25. Fear No Man's Sin..89
26. Not a Tragedy 93
27. Recalculating...96
28. Sadness Laced with Joy..100
29. His Eye Is on the Sparrow....................................103
30. Sniper Fire from the Enemy 105
31. Seeking God's Will 109
32. Shrink the Giant Dot 112
33. Sink or Swim 115
34. A Healthy Respect for I-65 118
35. Spiritual Mazes 121
36. The Grace of Giving 125
37. No Trespassing: Forbidden Territory...................128
38. The Winter of Our Content 131
39. Live in Harmony...135
40. A Child of the Wind 138
Thoughts from the Author 141

Other Writings

Who Gets the Credit? 145
Elizabeth 149
Single Women and Sexuality.....................................159
Building Up Your Husband..178
Teaching Children to Respect 187

Wisdom for Life
Devotional Series

The Wisdom for Life devotional series gives some older women an opportunity to share many of the truths, insights and analogies that have helped them and others through the years.

If sometimes you wish you could just sit down at the table across from a spiritual mom and hear some of the important things she has learned in her life, this is your chance.

Gloria Baird wrote the first volume, entitled *God's Pitcher*. This is the second volume, *My Bucket of Sand*, by Sheila Jones. In the years to come there will be more volumes, more wisdom, more "table talks" with women who have much to share.

Each volume will be unique because each woman, like you, is one of a kind.

We hope you will join us, and that, in the joining, you will gain "wisdom for life."

> Likewise, teach the older women to be reverent in the way they live, not to be slanderers or addicted to much wine, but to teach what is good. Then they can train the younger women to love their husbands

and children, to be self-controlled and pure, to be busy at home, to be kind, and to be subject to their husbands, so that no one will malign the word of God. (Titus 2:3–5)

My Bucket of Sand

How precious to me are your thoughts, O God!
    How vast is the sum of them!
Were I to count them,
    they would outnumber the grains of sand.
                                    Psalm 139:17–18

The thoughts of God are vast, uncountable, infinitely far reaching. As the Psalmist says, they outnumber the grains of sand. Have you ever tried to count teeny, tiny grains of sand?

God is gracious. He shares his thoughts with us. His people. His children. The citizens of his kingdom.

He who forms the mountains,
    creates the wind,
    and *reveals his thoughts to man*,
he who turns dawn to darkness,
    and treads the high places of the earth—
    the LORD God Almighty is his name.
(Amos 4:13, emphasis added)

Through his indwelling Spirit, the Lord God Almighty

opens up to us his heart, his mind, his plans, his dreams. And he doesn't view it as casting his pearls to the pigs. How loving of him. How trusting of him. How amazing of him.

> "No eye has seen,
>   no ear has heard,
> no mind has conceived
>   what God has prepared for those who love
>   him"—
>
> but God has revealed it to us by his Spirit.
>   The Spirit searches all things, even the deep things of God. For who among men knows the thoughts of a man except the man's spirit within him? In the same way no one knows the thoughts of God except the Spirit of God. We have not received the spirit of the world but the Spirit who is from God, that we may understand what God has freely given us. This is what we speak, not in words taught us by human wisdom but in words taught by the Spirit, expressing spiritual truths in spiritual words.
>   (1 Corinthians 2:9–13)

Are we grasping this? No one knows the thoughts of God except the Spirit. And then…we have received the Spirit who is from God. So the Spirit, who lives inside us, reveals the thoughts of God to us. He is the only one who knows them, and he is commissioned to share them.

When I consider the thoughts of God—those uncountable grains of sand—I feel like a barefoot child walking on the beach with the shoreline stretching as far as I can see. I am carrying a small bucket with me that is full of sand. The sand is in my bucket, but it isn't mine; it comes from the boundless store that is all around me.

Any thoughts that are true are first his thoughts. The sand in my bucket is his sand. In this book I am sharing with you some of the sand God has graciously put in my bucket.

Connecting the Dots

Remember when you, or your kids, labored over connect-the-dots pictures? You took your pencil point from dot to dot, and then finally, ta-dah, there it was: a picture of something you could recognize.

But think about a connect-the-dots picture that has too few dots that are spaced too far apart. Your pencil meanders between dots, inventing a whole new picture than the artist had in mind. Maybe you come up with a wagon, but what was intended was a school bus. You need enough dots close together to draw an accurate picture.

How often do we do this in life situations? That is, we have a few life "dots," and since we can't see the big picture, we put them together in a way that makes sense to us.

We don't realize that our big picture is lacking dots, or perhaps the dots are spaced far apart, and therefore our picture is inaccurate.

For example, consider something that happened with my husband, Tom, and me recently. I came into his office and saw that he had printed out a picture of me and had placed it near his computer. Well, of course, it is sweet that he wanted to see my face while he was working. However, this picture was taken several years ago…maybe even as long as twelve years ago.

I took that one "dot" (the fact that he had printed an out-of-date picture of me and was displaying it), and I drew a picture that had all kinds of dips and turns. I asked myself: "Why did he print out a picture of me when I was younger? Did he want to look at that picture because I have now gotten older? Or did he wish I dressed up more for work like I used to when I went into the office every day (instead of dressing casually and working from home as I do now)? Did it bother him that some days I don't get presentable until later in the morning, so he wanted a picture of me looking all neat and together?"

After coming up with all these possible pictures from the one dot I was given, I did what I should have done: I asked the "author" of the dot why he had printed out a twelve-year-old picture of me. He simply said, "I have always liked that picture." That was it. The other hypotheses in my head were not accurate.

Years ago I read a book in which the author suggested that we employ the use of "rival hypotheses." For example, if you go to a church function one day, and just as you walk up to speak to someone, she turns and walks away.

You have one dot.

Then you take that one dot and draw a picture: "She saw me coming and didn't want to talk to me, so she turned her back and just walked away, leaving me standing there looking like a fool. She must not like me."

Now, take this hypothesis that you have come up with and explore some rival hypotheses such as: "You know, she might have had some things on her mind and was distracted. She might not have even seen me approaching her." Or "Someone once told me that she was hurt that I had ignored her, and I had no memory of the 'snub' that she described. I had been lost in my own world at the time and had nothing at all against the person."

After considering these rival hypotheses, we can feel better about the situation and not be so sure that our original dot-connecting was accurate. We might realize that we have done what Jesus told us not to: judge another person (Matthew 7:1).

Our fears might be put to rest by just doing this rival-hypotheses exercise, or we might need to go talk with the person to make sure she is okay with us. If we do talk with the person, we will be a lot more reasonable, a lot less emotional and hopefully not as judgmental because we know there are other possibilities than the one we first conjured up.

When we are willing to initiate with people to get more dots for our pictures, we will most likely be more accurate in our understanding and also be more at peace on the inside.

Apparently this is not a new phenomenon. Solomon had something to say about this tendency too:

> It is not good to have zeal without knowledge,
>   nor to be hasty and miss the way.
> (Proverbs 19:2)

We can be too quick and too zealous to connect our few dots, and do so without knowledge. In our hasty conclusion, we "miss the way"; our thoughts meander and we draw the picture inaccurately. Let's remember to slow down, use rival hypotheses, and extend grace to everyone, just as God does to us.

God, Don't Drop Me

My times are in your hands;
   deliver me from my enemies
   and from those who pursue me.
                                    Psalm 31:15

Our youngest daughter, Corrie, was born with a congenital heart defect called transposition of the great vessels. Twelve hours after delivery she had to be flown to St. Louis Children's Hospital, four hours away by car. As I tearfully told her good-bye in the neonatal nursery, I began to worry that one of the nurses might drop her during the journey. She was so tiny and vulnerable.

My mothering instincts were strong. If I were with her, I would be holding her and she would not be dropped! (This irrational belief is what my friend Marcia Lamb calls "momnipresence." If I am there, nothing will happen to my child.) But I could not be there—only the nurses were allowed to go.

Then I remember thinking, "If it is God's will for my baby

to make it to St. Louis, she will make it to St. Louis. There is nothing anyone can do to keep her from making it. But if it is not God's will for her to make it to St. Louis, there is nothing anyone can do to cause her to make it." It was clear to me that Corrie was in God's hands, and all I needed to do was trust.

Thankfully, she did make it, and the doctors did a procedure on her that enabled her to live until open-heart surgery could be performed a year later. She is a vibrant and healthy thirty-year-old young woman now, and we are very grateful!

This irrational fear of being "dropped" can also show up in our relationship with God. When life is challenging, we can become insecure and fear that God will drop us. Sometimes we believe he is big enough to create the world and the galaxies and the intricate balance of nature, but then think he is not able to hold on to us when the flight gets bumpy.

I can find myself trying to take hold of situations to make them work out right. Of course, "right" means the way I think they should work out.

I remind myself that God is holding me in his hands, his eternally capable hands. It is foolish to say I trust him but then live as if he is not worthy of that trust.

Truly my times are in his hands, and your times are in his hands. He will always hold on to us. And he will never drop us.

From One Goose to Another

It is a sure sign of fall: "Wild geese that fly with the moon on their wings."[1]

While on a prayer walk around my neighborhood, I saw their "V" formation slicing through the sky.

As I watched them, I was reminded of their innate wisdom given by God. I suppose most of us have read somewhere the benefits of flying in V formation as opposed to say X or Z formation.

One benefit that scientists put forth is that it conserves their energy. Each bird flies slightly above the bird in front of him, resulting in a reduction of wind resistance. Then they take turns being in the front position, falling back when they get tired. In this way, they can fly for a longer period before they have to stop for rest.

As Christians in community and relationship, we are

---

1. From the song "My Favorite Things" in the movie *The Sound of Music*.

much like these geese. Sometimes we are the one who flies in the front, asserting our faith as the rush of life comes at us. But sometimes we are the ones who are flying off the wing of a friend.

It brings to mind a conversation I had with a close friend. She told me that when she was first getting to know me, she had thought I might be "high maintenance." I bristled a bit to think that I would ever be considered high maintenance by anyone. I told her that my natural tendency if anyone ever thought that of me was to pull away, to show that I didn't need anyone, that I was a low-maintenance person.

She wisely replied, "We are all high maintenance at some point."

So true. (See 1 Corinthians 12:21–26.)

We were not created to always be the first goose. We take turns in that position. That is, if we are in touch with our own inadequacies, our own weaknesses, our own sin…we will fly off the wing of a friend from time to time. And we will be happy for them to fly off ours.

Special Gifts: A Hug and a Kiss

Now that you have purified yourselves by obeying the truth so that you have sincere love for your brothers, love one another deeply, from the heart.

1 Peter 1:22

During the past Christmas season, I was given a special gift. As I was going through some of my parents' old pictures stored in a cigar box, I came across one of my dad giving me a hug. I must have been around twenty-seven years old.

My father died of Alzheimer's disease in 1988, but I had lost him long before he breathed his last breath. The dad I knew did not know me when he died. Those who have experienced this disease know the pain it brings.

In this picture, it is very special to see my dad's strong arms around me and the sweet smile of contentment on my face. It reminds me of a moment that I had with him during the year before he died. He was in a nursing home, and I went to see him every day to make sure he was eating and that his needs were being met.

My mother had died a year before, so in many ways I already felt like an orphan. I remember that my dad was making some kind of movement with his face, and I couldn't tell what he wanted or what he was trying to communicate. So I bent closer to him and put my face up to his. Then I realized that he was puckering…he was trying to give me a kiss.

I put my cheek against his lips, and I marveled. Tears came to my eyes as I was given a gift I thought I would never again experience—a kiss from one of my parents. Even as I recount this to you now, tears come to my eyes. A last kiss from my sweet Daddy, who was gentle and kind, and who loved me so much.

I don't know what he thought or what he understood the day he gave me that kiss, but somehow I know that God was giving me this present to help me keep the memory of my dad alive in my heart.

This picture of him hugging me has the same effect.

I encourage you to hug those you love and to give them a kiss. These are the gifts that matter most.

Freedom in Christ

Isn't it cool how some truth spoken to you years ago stays in your head as if it had been said ten minutes ago?

I remember talking to Gloria Baird at a women's conference in Boston.[1] At the time, I had probably only seen her once before at another conference. But I had heard classes of hers on cassette tapes (remember what those are?), and I had thought that our voices sounded somewhat alike—the way we pronounced certain words. She was from Texas and I was from Alabama, so we both had a soft Southern lilt to our accent.

Anyway, I said to her that I had recently felt like a bird in a cage, chirping out to God over and over: "Set me free. Set me free. Set me free." As a Christian, I had still felt caught, trapped, bound in guilty feelings and fears.

I continued triumphantly: "But then I realized that in

---

1. Gloria is the author of the first volume of the Wisdom for Life series: *God's Pitcher*.

Jesus, God had opened the door of the cage. I was desperately repeating, 'Set me free,' and there right before me was an open door. All I had to do was fly out." Feeling freed up by this realization, I was pretty happy.

But Gloria very kindly looked at me and said, "Sheila, the truth is, there isn't even a cage."

In Jesus, God had not just opened the door; he had removed the cage:

> Therefore, there is now no condemnation for those who are in Christ Jesus, because through Christ Jesus the law of the Spirit of life set me free from the law of sin and death. (Romans 8:1–2)

Are you allowing guilt from forgiven sins or cruel accusations from Satan or negative thoughts about yourself to rob you of your peace? If so, you too need to remember: you are free. There is no cage. "There is now no condemnation for those who are in Christ Jesus."

Don't Freeze-Frame

The other day I was looking at a picture of Tom taken about five years ago in a park. My eyes were drawn to the background where I saw a child wearing blue jeans and a red shirt. He was running—frozen in the posture of pumped arms and legs.

Though he was moving quickly, though he had assumed many different poses within a few seconds' time, in this photograph he will always be in this position—trapped—captured—no escape—freeze-framed.

Though he will change clothes many times in his life, in this photograph he will always wear blue jeans and a red shirt—trapped—captured—no escape—freeze-framed.

With each other, we can freeze-frame a hurtful action, a senseless statement, a stupid idea. Then forever in our minds, this is who that person is. He or she is character-ized by the snapshot of that moment.

And yet there are so many more moments in a person's life that define them fully. Millions of frames in the moving picture of their grace-filled, imperfect life—times of great sacrifice and love, times of noble deeds and insightful comments, times of deep faith and strong conviction.

I don't want to be freeze-framed in anyone's mind. And I don't want to freeze-frame anyone else. Sometimes we don't even know we have done it—that we have judged someone on the basis of frozen evidence.

I am so grateful that God does not freeze-frame me when I am being prideful, or when I am being selfish or jealous. Through the grace of Jesus, he lets the picture keep mov-ing and forgives me as I go. I am never trapped or cap-tured in my sin.

Let's not freeze-frame each other. Let's start the action and let people move on in our minds—let them continue to grow, mature, change…and be forgiven.

> Speak and act as those who are going to be judged
> by the law that gives freedom, because judgment
> without mercy will be shown to anyone who has not
> been merciful. Mercy triumphs over judgment!
> (James 2:12–13)

Canned or Fresh

Have you ever had any experience with canning vegetables? Once a long time ago, in another galaxy far, far away, I decided I was going to be Mrs. Domestic and can some green beans. I had two small children at the time, and it was a little nerve-wracking for me to keep a watch on the canner's pressure gauge.

For those to whom this practice seems like something out of *Little House on the Prairie*, when you can vegetables in this fashion, you use a specialized pressure cooker partially filled with water. You put the jars inside the pot, and place it on the burner. Then you build the internal heat and pressure to a certain point to sterilize and seal the jar tops, giving the assurance of no bacteria inside the jars.

If you don't watch the gauge, the whole thing could blow your house next door or down the street or to the moon. Well, a little bit of exaggeration, but it could blow up anyway. This is not something you want to happen while your toddler is coming into the kitchen to ask for a drink of water.

For you young urbanites who are reading this: many years ago, people planted gardens, picked the ripe vegetables, and then canned them for use during the winter. Mason jars were lined up in the pantry ready to feed the family. In the midst of the current "green" movement, some are re-embracing this retro practice.

In thinking about the canning process, it occurred to me that while in conversation with someone, I was willing to be very open about past experiences in my life that were, so to speak, already "canned." I was happy to go get those Mason jars of experience off the shelf and open them up and share honestly about them. I knew the outcome of those situations. They didn't threaten me. They didn't make me feel as vulnerable as something I was currently going through.

Wouldn't you agree that in sharing about our lives with someone else, it is easier to talk about what has happened and is finished? It is more difficult to talk about something "in progress," something that has not been neatly and safely worked through yet, something that makes us feel insecure or out of control…basically, something not yet sealed and canned.

It is so much easier to share from our strengths, from our victories, from our "done deals." But we need to stretch our humility and our trust, and be willing to share a current situation that is far from being resolved.

Now, please don't misunderstand me: we *should* be sharing what we have learned from our past. We would be stingy not to do this. Wisdom is borne from such experiences as these. And wisdom is to be passed on, not to be hoarded. This is why Paul calls on the older women to train the younger women in areas of life they have already experienced and learned from (Titus 2:3–5).

My epiphany was that sharing my thoughts should include a mixture of canned and fresh, known and unknown, past and present. I don't need to always have the answers; I just need to trust the one who does.

Let's say I am talking with someone who is having some frustrations in a certain area of her life. I can go into my mental pantry and pull down several canned experiences to help and encourage my friend. This is good and right to do. But this doesn't necessarily mean that I am sharing my heart with her. I need to also be willing to be vulnerable about my life—my current temptations, fears and hurts—not just have answers for people out of my past experiences. I don't want to come across as someone who has it all together…because I surely do not.

We are all works in progress, and we daily need the help and guidance of the Spirit. We need to keep learning, sharing and imitating the humble heart of our Lord:

> All of you, clothe yourselves with humility toward one another, because,

> "God opposes the proud
>   but gives grace to the humble." (1 Peter 5:5b)

Do Not Be Anxious

Rejoice in the Lord always. I will say it again: Rejoice!
Let your gentleness be evident to all. The Lord is near.
Do not be anxious about anything, but in everything,
by prayer and petition, with thanksgiving, present
your requests to God. And the peace of God, which
transcends all understanding, will guard your hearts
and your minds in Christ Jesus.

Philippians 4:4–7

In the past, I didn't consider myself a very anxious person. In fact, I didn't relate very well to those who were. But as I have gotten older, I have found myself becoming more anxious.

Maybe I have seen and heard too much about bad things that have happened to people. I saw the statistic that our children receive in the span of a few months the same amount of information that our grandparents were aware of in their lifetime. This is also true about our awareness of tragedies that happen all over the world. Grandparents of the baby boomers didn't have real-time CNN breaking news of train wrecks in Spain, terrorist attacks in Iraq, earthquakes in India, small plane crashes in Houston, Interstate pile-ups in Denver, and a rape in South Carolina.

There is also a new syndrome called "cyberchondria," which results from people searching the Internet to find the cause of their health symptoms. By the time they finish their research, they are convinced they are most likely dying. Meanwhile their blood pressure is going sky high, and they are hyperventilating, which can confirm the assumed about-to-die diagnosis.

Sometimes when I go to bed at night, I look forward to nestling my head into my memory-foam pillow and drifting off to sleep. But then they come—those worrisome thoughts that rob me of my peace, cause anxiety and delay the release of my body's rest-producing melatonin.

These thoughts can take the form of tragedies that *almost* happened in the past. My mind will replay them—over and over—showing me what would have happened if they had come to fruition. Or I can relive terrible things that happened to people I don't even know, that I read about or heard on the news. I have a long list of those that I will not tell you (to save you from their visits in your head too!).

And the dreaded "what ifs" want their playtime too.

Can you relate to what I am saying? We are aware of so much tragedy, and we insert ourselves, our husbands, our friends, our children, and even our pets into the place of others who have had these experiences.

Add to this the economic uncertainty, the pressures of work, childrearing, the newest strain of flu and any other number of stress-inducing factors, and we are set up for anxiety attacks and a generally agitated state of mind.

Enter stage right: pushing his way through the crowd of thoughts gathered on the stage of our minds—the Holy Spirit through Paul says: "Do not be anxious about anything." Is this realistic? Is it a pipe dream? Was it only a possibility in the slow-moving first century? These are real questions that we have to ask ourselves if we are being completely honest.

I have been reading a book titled *Calm My Anxious Heart*. It was very popular ten or so years ago, but I didn't pay much attention to it. Remember…I didn't deal with much anxiety then. When I picked up the book last weekend, I was feeling very anxious, in fact, irrationally anxious, about several things.

I realized that in the past I was relying too much on

myself and not enough on God. I was younger. I was stronger. I had more natural confidence and can-do spirit. Now I am older and not quite as physically and emotionally resilient. I am more aware of anxiety, and I feel weaker and less able to deal with it.

Therefore, I understand more than ever how much I need God to be my strength.

God said to Paul, "My grace is sufficient for you, for my power is made perfect in weakness" (2 Corinthians 12:9). I have read it, taught it, believed it and applied it to a certain extent, but now I need to go deeper.

Anxiety is very strong.

I am grateful that God is stronger still.

When anxiety is rising in me, I remind myself: "God is either in control or not. I must choose to believe one way or the other, and then live as if that belief is true. I choose to believe that God is in control."

In *Calm My Anxious Heart*, Linda Dillow writes of coming to much the same conclusion I had come to:

> Contentment is accepting God's sovereign control over all of life's circumstances. It was humbling for me to have to say to God, "I've tried to trust you, but

too much of my own strength has been mixed with that trust."[1]

Also, what she reminded herself was the same thing I reminded myself: God is in control. She quotes 1 Timothy 6:15 from the Phillips translation:

> God...is the blessed controller of all things, the king over all kings and the master of all masters.

I love that description of God: "the blessed controller."

To help myself start the day remembering to rely on my Blessed Controller, I came up with a little rhyme that I repeat when I wake up:

A new morning,
a new day.
Rely on God
in every way.

1. Linda Dillow, *Calm My Anxious Heart* (Colorado Springs: NavPress, 1998), 17.

Keep on Walking

For though we live in the world, we do not wage war as the world does. The weapons we fight with are not the weapons of the world. On the contrary, they have divine power to demolish strongholds. We demolish arguments and every pretension that sets itself up against the knowledge of God, and we take captive every thought to make it obedient to Christ.

2 Corinthians 10:3–5

Have you ever been tyrannized by bizarre thoughts that keep coming into your mind? The more you try to push them out the door, the more they come in through the windows? They might be of a sexual nature, a violent nature, a profane nature or you-name-it. You hate them and don't want to think them, and yet, there they are, setting up housekeeping in your brain. They are unwelcome guests who are intent on homesteading your mind.

This maddening type of experience has been mine. It is the old "don't think of a white bear" syndrome. The more we try not to, the more he keeps tromping around in our minds.

We know that Paul talks about taking every thought captive, and we know that we want to put our "white bear" in a cage and ship him off to parts unknown. We also know that we have "weapons" from the Holy Spirit for taking such thoughts captive: reading God's word (Ephesians 6:17), praying (Ephesians 6:18), bringing the thought into the light (1 John 1:7), confessing any sin that would feed it (1 John 1:9), taking a stand against it (Ephesians 6:13) and calling on the power of the Holy Spirit to protect us as we put on the full armor of God (Ephesians 6:11).[1]

But many of us might have the following experience: When we try to use these weapons, they don't seem to be successful because the thoughts are still there. We know the weapons themselves are not defective because they are from God. So we figure we just don't know how to use them properly. We end up feeling guilty and at the mercy of our errant thoughts.

---

1. Note that the word translated "weapons" can either refer to offensive tools, such as the "sword of the Spirit," or to defensive accoutrements such as the "full armor of God."

I want to share with you an analogy that has helped me when my mind gets stuck on some type of bizarre thought.

Imagine that you are standing on a street corner with a bunch of really rough characters. They are using obscenities right and left. You hate hearing all this trash. You try to cover your ears, but you can still hear it.

Then, you make the decision: "I am going to walk away. I don't want any part of this scene." Your walking away infuriates them, and they began screaming their obscenities after you. You are hearing them even more clearly than you had when you were standing on the corner.

You feel defeated. You had made a clear, faithful decision to walk away, and now these evil words are louder and more intense than ever. So, you say to yourself, "I might as well turn around and go back to the corner. I give up. I guess I will just have to live this way."

But the truth is that if you decide to keep on walking, even though it gets worse after you first make the decision, eventually you will get to your house, open your door, shut it, and leave the activities on the corner far behind.

❄

So, back to the bizarre thoughts that are bullying you. You feel helpless to gain control over these seemingly unruly thoughts. You decide, "I am just going to take a stand, to go about my life and say 'I don't want any part of you.'"

When you do that, the thoughts seem to get worse. You think, "Here I made a decision to put them behind me, but they are worse than ever. I give up."

Don't be surprised that it is worse right after you make that decision. You might even expect it to be.

When the thoughts come again, say to yourself: "I have already made it clear to God that I don't want any part of these thoughts. The Holy Spirit is active, moving to protect me. I have repented of anything I am aware of that might trigger these thoughts, so I am free. I can just ignore them when they come. I can laugh in Satan's face and say, 'God already has the victory. These are just parting shots from a defeated enemy.' I can declare and accept freedom, by faith, even though the thoughts are still there."

Then eventually, without even realizing how it happened, you will find yourself far away from those thoughts, safe in your "house," with the door shut. It takes courage to hold on to freedom when Satan's assaults continue.

❈

I believe that when Jesus had his showdown with Satan after his baptism in Matthew 4, he was not facing a cartoonish red man with a forked tail. I believe the attacks and the battle were in the form of thoughts in his mind.

He held his ground with each thought sent to tempt him. He countered with a statement of faith: "It is written…" And he held on to what God had said and what God had promised. He lived out what his brother James would write a few years later:

> Submit yourselves, then, to God. Resist the devil, and he will flee from you. (James 4:7)

James wrote it because Jesus had proven it.

It was after Jesus took a most decisive step in his walk with God, that Satan hit him hard with un-Godlike thoughts in his head. He knew that he was free not to accept them and not to own them, even though they came to his mind. Just having the thoughts was not sinful. If he had believed them and given in to them, he would have sinned. Praise God he never did.

So we need to follow in his steps. We need to

> be self-controlled and alert. [Our] enemy the devil
> prowls around like a roaring lion looking for someone
> to devour. (1 Peter 5:8)

Call on God, claim the promises of Scripture, exercise the weapons God gives you to combat Satan's mental forays. Then accept your freedom. Faith believes you have received victory even before your mind realizes it:

> Therefore I tell you, whatever you ask for in prayer,
> believe that you have received it, and it will be
> yours. (Mark 11:24)

Bottom line: In faith, in freedom, in peace…keep on walking.

Carried Along

We recently returned from a trip to Colorado to celebrate our fortieth wedding anniversary. The bed and breakfast we stayed in was called Riversong, aptly named for the small river that ran beside it, bubbling, gurgling and swirling along.

I go back in my mind's eye to another time we were in Colorado. We have pictures of our two oldest girls, Amy and Bethany, beside another stream of this sort—there are so many in this beautiful, rugged Rocky Mountain area.

I can still remember sitting beside that stream so many years ago and having my eyes transfixed on a leaf, caught in the strong, unyielding current. It was carried along, easily accepting the twists and turns and bobs and bobbles.

I thought "I want to be that leaf, allowing the current of God's Spirit to carry me wherever he wants me to go." The following words came to my mind, and have never left:

> I am caught
> in your Spirit.
> Do not ever
> let me go.

Surely it was concerning such thoughts as these that Martin Luther once said: "When the Holy Spirit preaches in your heart, write it down."

I believe the Holy Spirit did preach in my heart while I sat beside that stream, and I am now "writing it down." His message from the Father was clear: "Yield yourself to me; quit trying to be in control of everything; trust me. And I will bless you beyond your wildest dreams."

The NIV uses the phrase "carried along by the Holy Spirit" in 2 Peter 1:21 where he describes the way God's Spirit moved prophets to speak God's word:

> For prophecy never had its origin in the will of man, but men spoke from God as they were carried along by the Holy Spirit.

Though we are not writing Scripture, we are receiving deeper and deeper insights into the ones that have been handed down to us…and these insights come "as we are carried along by the Holy Spirit."

I want to live my life in response to God's Spirit with the same lack of resistance and sense of abandon that I saw in that current-directed leaf thirty years ago.

The Gift of Laughter

I love to laugh.
Loud and long and clear.
I love to laugh.
It's getting worse every year.

You might recognize these lines from the movie *Mary Poppins*. In this scene, Mary takes her charges, Jane and Michael, to visit her Uncle Albert, who has a laughter "problem." As he laughs, he floats up to the ceiling, and his merriment is so contagious that eventually Mary, her friend Bert, and the kids join him for tea while hovering in the air.

Laughter is not only contagious; it is also healthy. Research has shown the restorative power of endorphins, those feel-good hormones that are released into the blood stream not only when we laugh, but also when we *anticipate* laughing!

Tom told me of a radio interview about "laughing yoga."

In this unusual yoga class, they work on proper breathing techniques, but they do not practice the normal "downward dog" position and other classic approaches. The main thing they do is laugh.

The instructor said that people walk into the class and start laughing simply because that is the purpose of their coming together. She also said that we can force laughter even if we don't necessarily think something is funny. Our body doesn't know the difference between real and counterfeit laughter; it releases the endorphins anyway. And if you fake laugh, it will usually trigger the real thing.

Endorphins are a gift from God, and just as he sends his rain on the just and the unjust, he also sends endorphins into the bloodstreams of the faithful and the unfaithful. If anyone can enjoy the lift of laughter, how much more should God's children avail themselves of this gift?

The writer of Proverbs tells us that

> A cheerful heart is good medicine,
> but a crushed spirit dries up the bones.
> (Proverbs 17:22)

We cannot control much of what happens in life, but we can control how we respond to what happens. We can choose our view, look for the good, find fun in the tedium.

Endorphins are there for the taking.

Maybe you have seen the "Debbie Downer" skits that the Saturday Night Live cast performed. My favorite is "Debbie Downer at Disney World." The family had come together for a reunion, and everyone was excited to ride the Haunted Elevator, to hug Tigger, and to see the Country Bear Jamboree…everyone, that is, except Debbie Downer. She preferred to talk about how feline AIDS is the number one killer of domestic cats and how Pluto would probably suffer heat stroke in the costume he was wearing, that is, if he avoided a terrorist attack, which was quite likely at a theme park.

Do we have a little bit of Debbie Downer in us? Do we sometimes focus more on the negative happenings than on the positive? It is up to us to decide. Both are always with us; we decide which controls our thinking.

The wise lady from Proverbs 31 "can laugh at the days to come." I don't know if that means she is not afraid of the future, or if she actually lets out a belly laugh now and then. I like to think it is both.

I remember when I was in the fifth grade, and autograph

books were all the rage. We mostly wrote silly, meaning-less rhymes to each other such as

> Roses are red.
> Violets are blue.
> You look like a monkey
> and smell like one too.

And

> When you get married
> And have twins,
> Don't come to my house
> For safety pins.

More meaningfully, I can still see my mother's handwriting on one of the pastel-colored pages as she wrote the Proverbs 17:22 passage, quoted earlier, from the King James Version:

> A merry heart doeth good like a medicine:
>> but a broken spirit drieth the bones.

I have fond memories of my mom and dad laughing together. My sister, Emily, and I grew up feeling free to laugh…as anyone who knows either of us will tell you. Laughter is a legacy. Certainly it is not as important as faith, but it is a great companion to faith.

Let's remind each other not to get so grown up, so busy

and so serious that we forget to exercise the gift of laughter. In fact, I encourage you to try it right now before you go on to the next chapter.

Lift the Other Foot

What do you think would happen if, when you went to bed at night, you kept one foot on the floor in case the bed were to fall? How much good rest do you think you would get?

When we get into our bed, we have to make the decision to either trust the bed to hold us up or to trust ourselves.

This is the way it is with trusting God. We can see how foolish it is not to lift the other foot when we go to bed. But do we see how foolish it is to not totally trust God, to keep one foot on the floor so we can handle things ourselves in case he doesn't come through?

Just as we have to put our full physical weight on the bed in order to rest, we have to put our full spiritual weight on God in order to be at peace.

I am coming to realize that I cannot be self-reliant and at the same time be God-reliant. I must choose. The choice of one will cancel the other. My prayer is that I, and you, will choose wisely—to rely on God and not on ourselves.

I am also realizing that my belief in the power of prayer is in direct proportion to the giving up of my self-reliance. If the tenor of my life is self-reliance, then prayer will not be the tenor of my life.

Isaiah was concerned about this same human tendency:

> Woe to those who go down to Egypt for help,
>   who rely on horses,
> who trust in the multitude of their chariots
>   and in the great strength of their horsemen,
> but do not look to the Holy One of Israel,
>   or seek help from the Lord. (Isaiah 31:1)

Tonight when you go to bed and lift the other foot, remember your need to totally rely on God.

NOTE: Credit to Hannah Whitall Smith for the bed concept in her book *The Christian's Secret of a Happy Life* (New York: Revell, 1952).

The Wilma Vitamin

When my kids were young, I gave them a daily Flintstone vitamin. Amy, the oldest, always wanted Wilma, and you know how it is when the oldest thinks something is cool: the others want it too. The best I remember, the vitamin bottle was populated by Fred, Wilma, Barney, Betty and Dino. This was the early 80s, and though Pebbles and Bamm-Bamm were already characters, they had not yet achieved vitaminhood.

Obviously I could not buy a whole bottle of Wilma vitamins, so it became a problem when all the Wilmas were used up. I could see the possibility of daily "I want Wilma" tantrums. So, I made a new vitamin rule: Each child had to take whichever character came out when I shook the bottle for their vitamin. If they got Wilma, it was just their lucky day.

As adults, we can be like this sometimes. That is, if someone else has something, we want it too. Maybe before they had it, we did not even consider that we needed it. But now we need it!

- A kitchen utensil that will make our life easier, even if we only use it twice a year

- A rolling stool for planting flowers, even though we seldom get around to this task

- The newest sneaker fad, even though our old ones are still quite functional

We see this trait of human nature in the movie *The Gods Must Be Crazy*. A pilot was drinking a Coca-Cola while flying low over the South African bush country. When he finished the last gulp, he opened his window and threw the glass bottle out. It landed unbroken near a bushman name Xi, who assumed the strange object was a gift from the gods.

Up until this point, the bushmen in his desert tribe had been content. They were thankful to the gods for giving them everything they needed to survive. This new gift became an object that they all found a use for. Everyone wanted it—so jealousy and envy grew.

❄

In the first century, the same tendency was operative. Paul addresses it in 1 Timothy 6:6–8:

> But godliness with contentment is great gain. For we brought nothing into the world, and we can take nothing out of it. But if we have food and clothing, we will be content with that.

Whether a Wilma vitamin, a kitchen utensil, a Coca-Cola bottle…no "thing" on this earth will bring us contentment.

Paul is such a great example for us. Listen, as he shares his heart:

> I am not saying this because I am in need, for I have learned to be content whatever the circumstances. I know what it is to be in need, and I know what it is to have plenty. I have learned the secret of being content in any and every situation, whether well fed or hungry, whether living in plenty or in want.
> (Philippians 4:11–12)

And what is this secret?

> I can do everything through him who gives me strength. (v13)

His relationship with Jesus. His trust in God. His reliance upon the Holy Spirit.

If we really want to get ahead in life, instead of clamoring for things, let's clamor for godliness. "Godliness with contentment is great gain." Let's be content no matter which vitamin comes out of the bottle.

15

God-Breathed

I love the imagery in the Greek word *theopneustos*, translated in the NIV as "God-breathed." Paul says to Timothy, his son in the faith:

> All Scripture is God-breathed and is useful for teaching, rebuking, correcting and training in righteousness, so that the man of God may be thoroughly equipped for every good work. (2 Timothy 3:16–17)

"All Scripture is God-breathed."

It is the breath of a person that indicates and communicates "life." If you are breathing, you are alive. It has been so from the very beginning:

> The LORD God formed the man from the dust of the ground and breathed into his nostrils the breath of life, and the man became a living being. (Genesis 2:7)

The Scriptures impart to us the breath of God, the life of

God, the essence of his being. In and out, day and night, forever and ever—the eternal breath of God.

When we lived in New England, we had many cold days…many very cold days. On those days, if we were outside, we saw the presence of our breath in the form of a cloud of condensation in the air. We could just look at another person and know immediately whether he or she was alive. We could actually *see* their breath.

I like to think of the Bible as being the breathed-out Word on a cold day. You can actually see God's breath, his life, in the Bible. It is not nebulous. It is real and clear and discernable. Through the Bible, the Spirit blows the breath of God into our lives, just like paramedics performing CPR.

Breath is powerful. It is life-bringing and life-sustaining.

As he originally breathed life into the lungs of all the living, so God longs to breathe the life of his Spirit into all the living.

The next time you hold a Bible in your hand and open it, feel the breath of God—sometimes gentle and reassuring, other times bold and convicting.

Our God is an awesome God!

16

Getting Rid of Darkness

Years ago, I brought home a children's book from the library to read to my kids. It is the story of an old lady named Hildilid who lives alone, high in the hills.[1] She hates the night, and as soon as the darkness descends upon her, she tries to get rid of it by capturing it in a sack, tying it up with vines, boiling it, shaking her fist at it, and various other ineffectual approaches.

She is so exhausted by her nocturnal efforts that just as the sun begins to rise, she falls fast asleep, rests all day, and has renewed energy for her fight with the next night.

She didn't understand that the only way to dispel the darkness is to turn on the light. Hildilid's physical efforts had no power over the darkness; it was of a different realm, from an altogether separate sphere.

1. Cheli Duran Ryan (author) and Arnold Lobel (illustrator), *Hildilid's Night* (New York: Aladdin, 1996).

Sometimes we too try to rid our lives of darkness, or sin, in ways that are ineffectual. We ignore it and hope it goes away. We rationalize it and try to prove that it really isn't sin. We perform all kinds of good deeds in an effort to do penance and set our conscience free. But none of these approaches has any power over sin or any ability to absolve it and bring us into freedom.

The only way to rid our lives of darkness is to walk in the light:

> If we claim to have fellowship with him yet walk in the darkness, we lie and do not live by the truth. But if we walk in the light, as he is in the light, we have fellowship with one another, and the blood of Jesus, his Son, purifies us from all sin. (1 John 1:6–7)

We have to humbly enter the spiritual realm, the realm of Jesus and his sinless life being sacrificed for our forgiveness:

> Once you were alienated from God and were enemies in your minds because of your evil behavior. But now he has reconciled you by Christ's physical body through death to present you holy in his sight, without blemish and free from accusation. (Colossians 1:21–22)

> If we confess our sins, he is faithful and just and will forgive us our sins and purify us from all unrighteousness. (1 John 1:9)

How freeing it is to know that we can live as "children of light," and this is not a 60s, flower-power phrase; it is straight from the Holy Spirit:

> For you were once darkness, but now you are light in the Lord. Live as children of light (for the fruit of the light consists in all goodness, righteousness and truth) and find out what pleases the Lord. Have nothing to do with the fruitless deeds of darkness, but rather expose them. For it is shameful even to mention what the disobedient do in secret. But everything exposed by the light becomes visible, for it is light that makes everything visible. This is why it is said:
>
> "Wake up, O sleeper,
>   rise from the dead,
> and Christ will shine on you." (Ephesians 5:8–14)

Let's "wake up" daily and deal with darkness God's way. Let's have a humble, contrite spirit and rejoice that Jesus "called [us] out of darkness into his wonderful light" (1 Peter 2:9). Let's learn from Hildilid's ineffectual efforts and resolve to live as "children of the light."

17

I Don't Need Any Help

Before his downfall a man's heart is proud,
but humility comes before honor.

Proverbs 18:12

When my girls were toddlers, they would reach a stage of independence in which they would adamantly say, "Me do it!" Some task that they had gladly let me perform the day before, they were now determined to do on their own: put their socks or shoes on, feed themselves or put their clothes on. Sometimes the task was way beyond their ability, but they thought they could do it and strongly resented any help from Mom.

In the same way, a deep vein of independence runs through my old nature. Somehow, through the years, I have thought that it is a sign of weakness not to be able to do something, and it was a sign of strength not to need someone's help. So, bring on life; I can handle it.

It occurred to me one day that, in me and in some others I knew, there is the tendency to live our lives in a way that

63

nonverbally announces to everyone, "I don't need any help." But then, when we get in over our heads, we are quick to blame others for not helping us.

It is as if we are processing this way: "I don't need any help. I don't need any help. I don't need any help. How come nobody's helping me?!" We never even gave anyone a chance to help us. We went from independence to blaming, but skipped the step of vulnerability. We never gave a signal to anyone that we needed help. How were they to know that we had turned on a dime?

For example, you have a sick child, your husband is out of town, and the laundry room has flooded for the second time in two months. Before the bubbly deluge, a friend had said, "Could I bring you a meal tonight?" And you had said, "No. I'm fine. I have stuff I can fix." But after the flooding, you are standing there, mopping up the floor in your rain boots, crying and hungry. You feel all alone and sorry for yourself, and you think, "Why isn't someone helping me?" Later that night, a friend calls and you say, "We are just not a family in this church. My kid is sick, my husband is out of town, my laundry room is flooded, and I had to handle it without any help from anyone."

You forgot that your friend had offered to bring dinner over earlier. And you forgot that you didn't ask anyone to help you with the mopping—no one even knew about the mess you were cleaning up.

A good friend of mine tells about what happened when she was going through chemotherapy for breast cancer. People offered to help by cleaning her house or bringing food or doing anything else she needed. She had rebuffed them all, thinking she was strong enough to do these things and didn't want to be a bother to anybody else. Then she realized she was not able to keep up with the physical demands in her weakened state. She also realized that she was denying her friends the joy of serving her.

It is often pride that causes us to think we don't need any help, and it is often that same pride that then blames others for not helping us. Pride simply does not want to be humble. Humility realizes we do need help and allows us to ask for it.

> Humble yourselves before the Lord, and he will lift you up. (James 4:10)

18

Joy on the Journey

We have all heard stories about people who, wanting to be helpful, have picked up hitchhikers. Then the deceived driver was robbed, killed or raped, or all three. These tragic stories chill our bones and make us very aware of the dangers of allowing hitchhikers into our cars...especially since we are women and more vulnerable to attack.

I want us to be aware of other hitchhikers—those who show up unexpectedly as we are on our journey through life. They are standing along the side of the highway, thumbs out, eager to join us. You know some of their names:

Anxiety
Worry
Bitterness
Fear
Faithlessness
Hate

Against your better judgment, have you ever stopped the car and let any of them hop into the front seat with you? I have. They aren't just looking for a ride; they are set on stealing our joy and destroying us.

Because of his promise to be with us every inch of the way, God doesn't want us to pick up these ne'er-do-well hitchhikers. He wants us to have unimpeded joy on our journey, or "path," through life:

> You have made known to me the path of life;
>   you will fill me with joy in your presence,
>   with eternal pleasures at your right hand.
> (Psalm 16:11)

> But let all who take refuge in you be glad;
>   let them ever sing for joy.
> Spread your protection over them,
>   that those who love your name may rejoice in
>   you. (Psalm 5:11)

> The precepts of the LORD are right,
>   giving joy to the heart.
> The commands of the LORD are radiant,
>   giving light to the eyes. (Psalm 19:8)

Certain times in life we might have a stronger temptation to pick up the aforementioned hitchhikers. We are more vulnerable to being anxious and worried, to having fear and faithlessness, to giving in to bitterness and even hatred.

We understand that God wants to give us joy on our journey. But what about those times, we ask, when the feel-good endorphins mentioned in chapter 12 are not easy to come by? When jokes and funny stories are not appropriate? When life brings heartache and hurts? When there are curves and bumps and swerves and detours on our way? Where is the joy then?

Challenging times come to us all. They surprise us, take us unawares: disease, depression, death, divorce, difficult relationships—and those are just some of the "Ds"; there are many more challenges.

When I was in my mid-thirties, my journey was a heavy one. My mom had just died of gastrointestinal bleeding; my father, who no longer recognized me, was in a nursing home with Alzheimer's and I went to be with him daily (he died two years later); my husband had progressive MS and at the time was in the middle of a deep depression (which he talks about in his book *Mind Change*[1]); one of my daughters was at a very crucial time in her teenage life; I had two other daughters who need-

---

1. Thomas A. Jones, *Mind Change* (Spring Hill, TN: DPI, 1997, 2007).

ed me, and I was trying to help Tom lead a group of people in the ministry.

I had a lot on me. Where is joy when the journey bogs down like this?

I still found time for others, but I was also pushing myself emotionally and physically. It was tough to know exactly how to apportion my time and energies. These are times that you just keep putting one foot ahead of the other, trusting that somehow God is going to see you through. These are the times, as in the famous "Footprints" poem, that there is only one set of footprints in the sand...because God is carrying you.

Everybody will have hard times; they are part of the fabric of life. Those who have decided to follow Jesus learn and grow during these times. They get stronger because they learn to rely on God. As Peter, says, their faith is "proved genuine":

> In this you greatly rejoice, though now for a little while you may have had to suffer grief in all kinds of trials. These have come so that your faith—of greater worth than gold, which perishes even though refined by fire—may be proved genuine and may result in praise, glory and honor when Jesus Christ is revealed. (1 Peter 1:6–7)

True joy—of the deepest and most abiding type—comes through trusting God on our journey, even when it hurts. This is the undergirding type of joy that Jesus himself knew, and it is only in focusing on him that we can have this joy ourselves:

> Let us fix our eyes on Jesus, the author and perfecter of our faith, who for the joy set before him endured the cross, scorning its shame, and sat down at the right hand of the throne of God. (Hebrews 12:2)

Jesus made a promise to his disciples before his ascension, and he told them to pass on the promise to us:

> "Surely I am with you always, to the very end of the age." (Matthew 28:20)

We might say....to the very end of the journey. What a comfort to know.

It is my prayer that we, through Jesus, will hold on to our faith and our joy, and will not allow those hitchhikers—anxiety, worry, bitterness, fear, faithlessness, hate, or any others—to rob or destroy us.

19

For Their Sake

Do you have special and clear memories of Bible studies that you did years ago? A verse or a phrase that was emblazoned on your consciousness, to stay for a lifetime?

One such study for me was in the book of 1 Thessalonians...thirty years ago. I can see myself in the house with the 70s kitchen, complete with harvest gold appliances—the house that I almost burned down by leaving oil heating on the stove in anticipation of frying some breaded shrimp.

The sentence that has lodged with me all these years is at the end of verse 5 from chapter 1: "You know how we lived among you for your sake."

Here is the full context:

> For we know, brothers loved by God, that he has chosen you, because our gospel came to you not simply with words, but also with power, with the Holy

> Spirit and with deep conviction. You know how we lived among you for your sake. You became imitators of us and of the Lord; in spite of severe suffering, you welcomed the message with the joy given by the Holy Spirit. (1 Thessalonians 1:4–6)

Paul lived among the people for their sake, not for his own. He was focused on what was good for them, not what was good for him. He sacrificed his life to make theirs richer.

When I read that sentence, I stopped and thought, "Whoa! Am I doing that? Am I having that kind of heart for the people in my life? Am I living among them for their sake?"

Paul's heart called me higher. How natural it is to live among others, and be more aware of ourselves than of them. How unnatural it is to be more aware of them than of ourselves. It is the "unnatural" that is also the "spiritual."

Do I live among my family for their sake? Do I live among my neighbors for their sake? Do I live among my coworkers for their sake? Do I live among my brothers and sisters in the church for their sake?

Paul made it clear that he was emulating the character of Christ. And as he did so, he inspired those he lived among to do the same: "You became imitators of us and of the Lord" (v6).

Bottom line: I want that heart. I want to live among others for their sake. What a blessing that will be to their lives…and to my own.

20

Ever Feel Trapped?

Do you ever feel trapped in the mundane? In checking off your to-do list, getting the bills paid, the laundry folded, the shower cleaned, the grass mowed? Sometimes when days are flipping by in Rolodex fashion, I find myself sighing and feeling entrenched in the everyday-ness of life. The same-old same-old...

When this happens, though, I quickly remind myself how blessed I am to be able to wake up, to get ready, to do my work...to just be alive! The other day, I came across a little poem I wrote while in college. It went like this:

> A cricket chirped today
> But I gave it no ear.
> Will I have the privilege
> To hear one chirp next year?

A simple thought, but one that hit me in the middle of a normal, same-old kind of day. It made me want to appreciate the little things in life and not to take them for granted.

When I am feeling trapped by my everyday life, I also think about times I have been in the hospital, feeling sick and weak, getting stuck and pricked and poked. During those times, what I wouldn't give to just be able to be in my own bed at home or to be buying groceries or cooking dinner or weeding my garden—little things that mean so much when they are taken away.

The apostle John reminds us that "from the fullness of his grace we have all received one blessing after another" (John 1:16). Day after day, year after year, we receive one blessing after another. In fact, we are very pleasantly "trapped" in so many blessings.

Isn't it comforting to know that we will never find our way out of all these blessings?! Let's just decide to be grateful and to give God the praise he deserves:

> Surely you have granted [us] eternal blessings
> and made [us] glad with the joy of your presence.
> (Psalm 21:6)

21

Do Not Worry

Tom and I were recently with Christians in St. Louis for a weekend where he spoke about the power and meaning of the kingdom of God. When I spoke to the women on Saturday afternoon, I chose an aspect of kingdom living that I thought we all needed encouragement in: Jesus' injunction not to worry. (Matthew 6:25–34)

Some of the last words I shared were "I don't want to just teach about this…or to just talk about this. With God's help, I really want to do this!" Little did I know that God would give me an opportunity the very next day to practice what I had preached.

The motel we were staying in was close to the church building, so on Sunday morning I dropped Tom off early and went back to the room to load the car. It was hot and humid, and when I finished loading, I was winded.

I put the air conditioner on full blast and noticed I was

feeling some pressure in my chest. I just kept trying to get back to normal, taking some deep breaths. I went into the church building, hoping I would start feeling better. But as I sat in the pew, not participating in the song service, I realized I was feeling pressure coming up into my throat, and my hands and feet were feeling clammy.

Now, I had experienced these symptoms before and had been to the emergency room several times in the past twelve years. But even though each of those times the doctors said they could find nothing wrong, it is still disconcerting when these symptoms happen.

Thankfully my friend sitting next to me was a nurse, so I asked her to go out with me and to help me evaluate how I was feeling. She did, and brought another nurse.

Since my issues were classic heart attack symptoms, they encouraged, or insisted, that I go to the ER. I was resistant: "I have been here before. These symptoms will go away. I hate to make a fuss. I don't want to mess Tom up as he is about to speak."

Actually, I was being stubborn and a bit prideful. I was also putting them in a difficult situation. I had made them aware of the symptoms because I was concerned myself. Then I started to minimize the symptoms. As responsible medical professionals, they knew what needed to happen, but at first I was not a very willing patient.

I did, however, submit to them. We went to the ER, and the doctor kept me overnight. It ended up that neither the enzyme test nor the stress test (with EKG and nuclear imaging) showed anything. However, since I did have a symptom during the stress test (pressure in my throat), they put me on a beta-blocker and a baby aspirin and encouraged me to get a heart cath when we got back to Nashville.

I don't know the outcome at the time of this writing, but I do know that God very quickly gave me an opportunity to live what I was teaching: "Do not worry."

As I am facing my appointment with the cardiologist next week, I am going back over those notes on not worrying. I need them! Below is one of the points from those notes that I held on to.[1]

He Cares

During my senior year in high school, I worked at the A&P grocery store. They had a slogan: We Care. The employees wore big red buttons to prove it.

---

1. My doctor scheduled me for a heart cath, which showed my heart was in great shape. Very encouraging.

God isn't into "branding" and "marketing slogans," but he really does care. He has made this perfectly clear by sending Jesus to redeem us. Jesus didn't wear a button; he died on a cross.

Consider two passages that remind us of his ongoing care for us:

> Cast your cares on the LORD
> and he will sustain you;
> he will never let the righteous fall. (Psalm 55:22)

> Cast all your anxiety on him because he cares for you. (1 Peter 5:7)

When we are in his kingdom, on his team and part of his body, Jesus cares for us. Paul says it this way:

> After all, no one ever hated his own body, but he feeds and cares for it, just as Christ does the church—for we are members of his body. (Ephesians 5:29–30)

So, the all-powerful agent of creation calls us to follow him and to trust him…and he promises to feed and care for us.

"Therefore, do not worry."

22

Be Sympathetic

Finally, all of you, live in harmony with one another;
be sympathetic, love as brothers, be compassionate
and humble.

1 Peter 3:8

The Greek word for "sympathetic" connotes "experiencing pain jointly" or having a "fellow-feeling." To be truly sympathetic requires selflessness; it requires a willingness to suppress awareness of your own life, your own thoughts, your own pain, and put yourself in someone else's life, thoughts and pain.

Why would we want to do that? Why feel things we don't have to feel; why own things that life has not brought to our doorstep? As we share in the sufferings of others, we are imitating Jesus.

Some friends of mine began a ministry in which they offer a workshop entitled "From Hurt to Hope."[1] In this three-day interactive experience, the attendees learn to deal hon-

---

1. See www.caringresources.com.

estly and righteously with hurts from their past. And we all have hurts. There is no way to avoid them in this life.

The workshop helped me to identify some of the hurts I have felt and to make a decision to resolve them and move on. But I realized that many around me are carrying more baggage than I am.

I grew up in a loving Christian family and felt valued, affirmed and cherished. So many others did not have this blessing or opportunity. They have more baggage from their growing up years: a capricious alcoholic father, a promiscuous mother, an abusive brother, or critical and demeaning grandparents.

This thought came to me: The fact that I don't have as much baggage doesn't mean that I should just skip through the airport. If my friend has a whole conveyer belt of baggage, then I need to help carry hers. I need to be sympathetic, to experience pain jointly, to have a fellow-feeling.

This is what Paul tells the Galatians:

> Carry each other's burdens, and in this way you will fulfill the law of Christ. (Galatians 6:2)

Paul also tells us in 1 Corinthians 12 that when we are

part of the body of Christ, a phenomenon happens if we allow the Spirit to move in our hearts: one part suffers, and the other parts suffer with it.

If you hit your thumb with a hammer, your whole body sympathizes with that thumb, feels the pain, has a fellow-feeling. Your other hand grabs the thumb and strokes it. Your feet and legs cause you to hop up and down. You bend over and hold your hand into your body as if to cradle it and comfort it. Your voice box emits a low painful groan.

That thumb should never fear that it will suffer alone, in isolation, in disconnection.

Those who are members of Christ's body should never fear that they will suffer in isolation either. They should know that others will share in their suffering. This type of supportive unity among people from different backgrounds is unnatural, but it is real and is born only of the Holy Spirit of God.

Let us not quench the Spirit within us as God is trying to build "unnatural" unity in the body of Christ, his church. Reach out and carry someone else's baggage. It is amazing how much lighter your own will feel. Sharing our loads encourages us all.

23

No Fishing Allowed

In the 1970s I became a fan of Corrie ten Boom's book *The Hiding Place*, in which she tells her story of God's sustenance while in a German concentration camp during World War II. Her faith inspired and moved me. When I saw the movie that was made a few years later, I went to the restroom and sobbed. The vulnerability of the women who were captive to cruel guards disturbed my heart and shook my psyche. But in such a challenging situation, the faith of Corrie and of her sister, Betsy, called me higher.

Corrie was a woman who had a deep conviction about the absolute quality of God's forgiveness. Somewhere I read her response to the following passage from Micah:

> Who is a God like you,
>   who pardons sin and forgives the
>   transgression
>   of the remnant of his inheritance?
> You do not stay angry forever
>   but delight to show mercy.

You will again have compassion on us;
  you will tread our sins underfoot
  and hurl all our iniquities into the depths of
    the sea. (Micah 7:18–19)

She said that when God "[hurls] all our iniquities into the depths of the sea," he puts up a "no fishing" sign. Years ago, out to the side of this passage in my oldest Bible, I drew a little sign with wiggly, wavy lines of water underneath it: No Fishing Allowed. I need the reminder that when God forgives, he totally forgives. No fishing on our part. No diving. No dredging up those sins again. They are gone.

Corrie was released from the concentration camp due to a clerical error and lived to tell her story of God's faithfulness as she spoke to individuals and groups all over the world. It was Corrie's conviction that God tested her by putting her in a heart-stopping encounter with one of the guards who had been in her camp. The man came up to her after she had spoken to a group of people about her experiences. He reached out his hand to take hers and to ask her forgiveness.

Can you imagine the scenes that ran through her mind and replayed in her heart? Her father, sister, brother and nephew had all died in camps. And yet, she knew what Jesus said about forgiving others:

> For if you forgive men when they sin against you, your heavenly Father will also forgive you. But if you do not forgive men their sins, your Father will not forgive your sins. (Matthew 6:14–15)

Claiming the power of God to do what she could not do on her own, she reached out, took the man's hand—that same hand that had perpetrated such heinous crimes—and assured him of her forgiveness. Once again, Corrie's faith called me higher and taught me an even deeper lesson about God's forgiveness.

In response to Corrie's heart, let's ask ourselves: Has someone hurt me? Am I withholding forgiveness until they "earn" it? Am I willing to let go and let God help me forgive?

Remember, with our sins and theirs: No Fishing Allowed.

Keep the Welcome Mat Out

This is the message we have heard from him and declare to you: God is light; in him there is no darkness at all. If we claim to have fellowship with him yet walk in the darkness, we lie and do not live by the truth. But if we walk in the light, as he is in the light, we have fellowship with one another, and the blood of Jesus, his Son, purifies us from all sin.

If we claim to be without sin, we deceive ourselves and the truth is not in us. If we confess our sins, he is faithful and just and will forgive us our sins and purify us from all unrighteousness. If we claim we have not sinned, we make him out to be a liar and his word has no place in our lives.

1 John 1:5–10

Have you ever had a guest use your restroom, and when they left you realized to your horror that someone in your family had left a pair of underwear on the floor after their shower? Or the dog had pooped on the bathroom floor? Or…you fill in the horrid blank.

It gives you a helpless feeling, doesn't it? There is nothing you can do. You cannot clean it up, go back in time and rerun the action with the person coming into your perfectly ordered bathroom.

I realize that I want to present my house as I want to present my life—perfect.

But I realize there is often an "underbelly" to my house: the laundry room or back bedroom closet, for instance. I guide my guest to see only certain areas of my house; others are off limits. Those areas do not portray the neatness or the order that I want to be seen.

There is also an underbelly of my life. I don't like to show those parts. They are not as neat and clean and orderly as the parts I do want to show.

This is where John's injunction in the passage above comes in. He calls us as Christians "to walk in the light," to keep our lives open, to be real. If we act like we are perfect, we block the work of God in our lives. And we also hurt our fellowship with our brothers and sisters in Christ.

Who can relate to or connect with someone who is trying to prove he or she is perfect all the time? And why do we even want people to think that of us?

I sometimes want to come across as "all together" because I want people to like me, to think I am worthy of their friendship. The opposite is true. The more open and humble we are about our sins, our faults, our shortcomings, the more people are drawn to us. They realize we are just like them: flawed but forgiven children of God.

But it is precisely right in the middle of this underbelly that I can realize God's grace and that I will realize others' grace too…but only if I am willing to reveal these messier areas of my life.

Might some people judge me if they see the imperfection in my life? Yes, they will. But at that point, it becomes their problem…not mine. Most people will relate to those who expose personal weakness because they are all too familiar with their own.

This is a lesson I am trying to learn, but only in humility will I allow God to teach me.

I want to keep the welcome mat out…to my home and to my life. Come on in.

25

Fear No Man's Sin

Therefore, there is now no condemnation for those who are in Christ Jesus, because through Christ Jesus the law of the Spirit of life set me free from the law of sin and death. For what the law was powerless to do in that it was weakened by the sinful nature, God did by sending his own Son in the likeness of sinful man to be a sin offering. And so he condemned sin in sinful man, in order that the righteous requirements of the law might be fully met in us, who do not live according to the sinful nature but according to the Spirit.

Romans 8:1–4

Years ago I was trying to help a woman work through her challenging sexual past. Some of the situations she had been in were foreign to me; my old nature had not had these experiences. Many of my sins were insidious sins of the heart: pride, self-righteousness, jealousy. They were certainly as "bad" as her sins; sin is sin, and it separates us from God, apart from the sacrifice of Jesus.

As we talked, I assured her that not only was she forgiven of her sin, but she did not have to be a slave to the memory of it. "Through Jesus the law of the Spirit of life set [her] free from the law of sin and death." As we talked through her thoughts and temptations, we were going deep, and it was really dark—a place I didn't like to be. I had the fear that some of what she shared with me might give me problems, that it might leave me with thoughts that I also would have trouble getting rid of.

Then, a pithy statement came to me from the Holy Spirit: "Fear no man's sin." And best I remember, I told her, "I don't fear your sin."

How could I tell her that God had the power to set her free of her sinful thoughts if I didn't believe he had the power to set me free of anything I might "pick up" from her? If I was afraid the thoughts might trap me in some way, did I really believe that God could set her free?

I had to put my faith where my mouth was.

There are times we have to go to deep, dark places with people to help them be free of their sin.

The apostle Paul tells the Galatians:

> Brothers, if someone is caught in a sin, you who are spiritual should restore him gently. But watch yourself, or you also may be tempted. Carry each other's burdens, and in this way you will fulfill the law of Christ. (Galatians 6:1–2)

One of the ways in which the "restorer" might be tempted is what I mentioned above: She might have to deal with thoughts that were brought to her mind by the sin of the person she is trying to help. But it is in carrying each other's burden of sin that we fulfill the law (or principle) of Christ. Bearing this burden of sin is to follow in Jesus' steps.

Through the years, this understanding of "fear no man's sin" has helped me to make myself available to those who have cavernous hurts and seemingly unspeakable sins. I realize I, in my old nature, am capable of committing any sin.

Because of my upbringing and moral instruction, I avoided certain sins. But if I had the same upbringing and had been in the situations that some others were in, I most likely would have responded in the same way they did.

Back to my friend I mentioned earlier. I wanted her to know that each person's old nature consisted of different experiences, but all old natures are separated from God without the redemption of Jesus.

We are all in the same boat. Without Jesus, that boat is sinking. It doesn't matter whether you are in the front or the back of the boat, the end result is the same: you are sunk apart from him.

However, the great news is…

> There is now no condemnation for those who are in Christ Jesus.

26

Not a Tragedy

It was Easter several years ago. Our oldest daughter, Amy, had written a one-act play, a soliloquy from the perspective of Mary Magdalene, to perform at her church service that day. Tom and I were in another service on the other side of the Boston area, and I had come home to start the preparations for Easter dinner.

Amy called and said, "I was putting all my props in the trunk of the car, and I accidentally locked my keys in. Can you come and get me?"

There I was right in the middle of cooking. Most of the foods being prepared were ones I could not leave to cook on their own for the hour it would take to bring her a key. I would have to put dinner on hold, and then start again when I returned. I realized we were going to eat a very late Easter dinner that day.

My first inclination was to feel frustrated. But then I

thought, "If I had gotten a phone call that Amy had fallen off the stage and broken her neck during the performance today, that would have been a tragedy. However, this call that I got was just an inconvenience. I am not going to respond as if it were a tragedy."

Then, with a light heart and a calm demeanor, I drove to open Amy's trunk and retrieve her errant key.

I cannot tell you how this simple understanding has helped me since that time.

For example, if my car broke down when I was on my way to a very important appointment, I would think, "This is not a tragedy, just an inconvenience."

How often have we responded to an inconvenience as if it were a tragedy? And how often have we exploded on someone who was responsible for the inconvenience as if a full-blown tragedy had occurred and it was totally their fault? For all of us, the answer likely is: too many times.

We have all gotten calls that told us of tragedies: a death, illness, divorce, car accident. We know what it is to receive and to respond to such calls. But remember, when the matter at hand is not a tragedy, respond to it for what it really is: just an inconvenience. Be guided in your response by the fruit that comes from the Holy Spirit:

Not a Tragedy

The fruit of the Spirit is love, joy, peace, patience, kindness, goodness, faithfulness, gentleness and self-control. Against such things there is no law. (Galatians 5:22–23)

27

Recalculating

I have a trusty GPS that goes everywhere with me. I've given her the name Sally Forth, which means to "take off" or to "start out." Sally always knows where I am, even if I don't. And she always has a plan for the route I need to take to get from point A to point B.

Sometimes, though, for whatever reason, I do not go the way Sally has suggested. She says in her British accent, "Turn right," and I don't; I keep going straight. What I love about Sally is that she doesn't berate me or yell about how stupid I am for not going the right way. She very patiently says, "Recalculating." Amazingly, she remains patient even if I foil her plans several times in a row. Sometimes she will advise, "Make a U-turn as soon as possible."

God is somewhat like Sally. At times I don't go the way he has planned for me to go. I might be rebellious, or possibly I am clueless. If I miss a turn in my life, he is patient with me. If I have a humble spirit, he forgives me of my rebelliousness. And if I am simply clueless, he helps me know where to make a needed U-turn. I am thankful for his patience. As Peter says,

> Bear in mind that our Lord's patience means salvation. (2 Peter 3:15)

I am so thankful that as long as I keep looking to him, he never allows a wrong turn to ruin the rest of my life. He will still get me where I need to go.

When God was leading the children of Israel out of Egyptian bondage, he gave them a GPS system that was so large and so visible that they could all see it and follow:

> By day the Lord went ahead of them in a pillar of cloud to guide them on their way and by night in a pillar of fire to give them light, so that they could travel by day or night. Neither the pillar of cloud by day nor the pillar of fire by night left its place in front of the people. (Exodus 13:21–22)

God always knew where they were, even though they didn't. And he longed to take them to the land he had promised. Unfortunately, they decided they knew better, and they scorned his direction. Lacking a humble, repentant spirit, they forfeited the guidance of God. The whole adult generation that God had brought victoriously through the Red Sea ended up dying in the desert and not arriving at the destination they had started for. The only two of this generation who got to go into the promised land were Joshua and Caleb—the ones who had been humble and obedient before God.

This story of the Israelites is one of the Old Testament scriptures that Romans 15:4 says are written to teach us and that 1 Corinthians 10:11 says are written to be a warning and an example to us.

I said earlier that God was somewhat like Sally Forth. He is patient when I am repentant of my rebelliousness and when I am clueless about what he wants me to do. He works with me and gets me to the destination he has prepared for me.

But there is another way that God is not like Sally: He requires obedience and metes out consequences for disobedience. He is patient with us to bring us to repentance, and we need to respond with humility, not with pride or contempt:

> Or do you show contempt for the riches of his kind-
> ness, tolerance and patience, not realizing that
> God's kindness leads you toward repentance?
> (Romans 2:4)

Sally will continue to be patient no matter how rebellious I get. God will not. A time will come when I get to the end of his patience (when Jesus returns). I want to learn from the Israelites' mistakes so I will trust and obey him, and will seek his guidance daily in my life.

Then someday, just as Sally lets me know I have arrived by saying, "Destination on the right," he will say, "Well done, good and faithful servant. Welcome home."

28

Sadness Laced with Joy

There is a time for everything,
and a season for every activity under heaven:
a time to be born and a time to die,
a time to plant and a time to uproot,
a time to kill and a time to heal,
a time to tear down and a time to build,
a time to weep and a time to laugh,
a time to mourn and a time to dance...

Ecclesiastes 3:1–4

When my oldest daughter became thirty-six, I commented to a friend that I couldn't believe I had a thirty-six-year-old daughter. She jokingly replied, "Yeah. She's getting up there!" How much more am *I* getting up there?

Recently we pulled out our "archival" materials from the 60s and 70s and had them transferred to 21st century formats: slides to CD, audio cassette tapes and even reel-to-reel tapes to CD, and several 16-millimeter tapes to DVD.

We have now relived our wedding through audio. My voice was so quiet that we could not hear me say, "I do."

But we both know "I did."

We have a picture of me about to go out the door to the hospital to give birth for the first time. I am holding a checkbook in my extended right hand, and I have two fingers crossed.

We have watched our first child, Amy, crawling on the floor, bouncing in my lap, and walking unsteadily but exultantly on the orange/yellow shag carpet (gotta love the 70s).

It has been somewhat like passing through a time portal. How we wish we could do something about those horrific clothes and hairstyles, but they are what they are. No Photoshopping allowed. No revisionist history here.

I say all this to set the stage, to give background to the nostalgia that has come in the wake of these recent events.

Today I was walking down aisle three of the supermarket, and I watched a woman and her nine-year-oldish daughter walking toward me. Unbidden, tears came to my eyes. I flashed back to when my girls were younger, and we did everyday, ordinary things like go to the store. I didn't start bellowing or anything, but when I saw them again, my eyes misted once more.

Then, ten minutes later I was at the CVS, standing in the greeting card aisle, picking out valentines for my husband and daughters, and lyrics from the song playing on the overhead speaker got my attention: Stevie Nicks sang, "Children get older and I'm getting older too."

What is going on here? I think. *I get the point.*

I am in my early sixties. It's true: I am getting up there.

But you know, I am thankful for all these memories that were stirred with audio and video from the past. They bring a bit of sadness, but the sadness is laced with joy. And the joy settles in my heart. There is, indeed, a time and a season for everything.

29

His Eye Is on the Sparrow

I don't know how many of you are backyard birdwatchers. I most definitely am! My kids sometimes think I am crazy when they hear me excitedly exclaim something like, "I can't believe it; there is a pileated (pie-le-a-ted) woodpecker!!" (They are huge and look like cartoon characters with their high, flounced red headdress. If you have never seen one, you can google it.)

Once when I was looking out back to see what interesting birds might be visiting my feeder, I saw only sparrows—little brown, boring sparrows. It is always a bit of a letdown when only sparrows are munching around.

It then occurred to me how different God is from me. I want to look outside and see an indigo bunting (one of my favorite birds) or a blue grosbeak or a resplendent American goldfinch. I have never said to anyone, "Wow! Come here; come here! Look outside—over there on the feeder. Look. It's a sparrow!"

But God does say that. He doesn't require us to be the most interesting, the most beautiful, or the most unique to arouse his notice and his care. He looks out the window when we are at his "feeder," and he excitedly says to the angels, "Come here! Look! There is (fill in your name). Isn't she beautiful?!"

Jesus reminds us of how God takes care of the birds of the air—all of them, even the sparrow:

> "Look at the birds of the air; they do not sow or reap or store away in barns, and yet your heavenly Father feeds them. Are you not much more valuable than they?" (Matthew 6:26)

> "Are not two sparrows sold for a penny? Yet not one of them will fall to the ground apart from the will of your Father." (Matthew 10:29)

The next time you see a little brown, boring sparrow, remind yourself of the words from a popular song, "His eye is on the sparrow/and I know he watches me."

Rejoice! God is happy that we are at his feeder.

30

Sniper Fire from the Enemy

"You'll never be truly faithful."

"Something is wrong with you."

"You can't be pleasing to God."

"You are bad."

"You are fake."

"God could not love someone like you."

I think most of us hear negative, self-condemning thoughts like these in our heads at some point in our lives. Here is one way that I have used the Scriptures to combat these accusations from the enemy.

As a person who is seeking to be faithful to God, I am walking on the Highway of Holiness:

> And a highway will be there;
> it will be called the Way of Holiness.

> The unclean will not journey on it;
>> it will be for those who walk in that Way;
>> wicked fools will not go about on it.
>
> No lion will be there,
>> nor will any ferocious beast get up on it;
>> they will not be found there.
>
> But only the redeemed will walk there,
>> and the ransomed of the Lord will return.
>
> They will enter Zion with singing;
>> everlasting joy will crown their heads.
>
> Gladness and joy will overtake them,
>> and sorrow and sighing will flee away.
>
> (Isaiah 35:8–10)

I have chosen to take the journey of life on the King's Highway. While I travel there and hear the sniper fire of negative thoughts ringing out…from the left…from the right…from behind, I must understand that these are the attacks of the enemy. He is always lurking in the bushes, in the treetops, behind the rocks to accuse me (Revelation 12:10).

These thoughts he sends are negative, depressing, hopeless and especially prepared for and aimed at me. He knows my make-up, my past, my fears, my weaknesses, my thought patterns, and he capitalizes upon them. Another name for this sniper fire is "flaming arrows of the evil one" (Ephesians 6:16).

Into this analogy, I bring another scriptural understanding. I think of Saul on the road to Damascus. God brings a blinding conviction, a stop-life-as-it-is message directly from his heart to Saul's. While we are walking on the road, if God wants to show us changes we need to make, he has the power to do so. He does not engage in sniper fire that is difficult to trace down. He sends a "bright light" that stops us in our tracks. He brings conviction through the Holy Spirit.

What Satan wants us to do is to get off the Highway of Holiness and try to figure out where the shots came from. For example, we hear the thought, "There is no way you can be pleasing to God." We want to have spiritual integrity, so we think we should be open to this thought and receptive to being convicted of our sin. But this is a false accusation from Satan. He wants us to get off the path and chase illusive sightings of a spiritual sniper, knowing we will likely lose our way. And off the highway, Satan prowls as a roaring lion, eager to devour us.

The approach of a faithful pilgrim on the Highway of Holiness is to bring these accusations to God. To say,

> "Lord, if this is really from you, I know you can get my attention through your Spirit and through people in my life to bring me conviction, to help me

understand anything I need to see and to change. I trust that you have the power to reveal your truth in a clear way as you did to Saul in a shaft of light directly to his soul. Meanwhile, I am going to keep walking, staying on the highway, and not giving Satan a foothold in my life. There is no condemnation for those who are in Christ Jesus."

If God is able to speak the universe into existence, to make darkness and light, to raise the mountains and fill the seas, to work throughout history to bring about his plan of redemption through Jesus, then surely he is able to communicate truth to me in a way that shows it is clearly from him.

What should you do when these sniper-fire thoughts are zinging all around you?

Just continue to walk! Never leave the Highway of Holiness. Remember that only the redeemed can walk there, and you are redeemed. Continue to trust God to reveal his will to you. And you will walk directly into the safety of his arms.

31

Seeking God's Will

> Therefore, I urge you, brothers, in view of God's mercy, to offer your bodies as living sacrifices, holy and pleasing to God—this is your spiritual act of worship. Do not conform any longer to the pattern of this world, but be transformed by the renewing of your mind. Then you will be able to test and approve what God's will is—his good, pleasing and perfect will.
>
> Romans 12:1–2

I have talked with many women who are seeking to determine God's will in certain situations. And I have sought to do the same. A classic passage to offer will-finding help is Romans 12:1–2, seen above.

To find God's will, we first need to remember the great mercy he has shown us—his desire to give to us and meet our needs. Then, we willingly and thankfully offer ourselves as living sacrifices, trusting that his will is best for us—it is "good, pleasing and perfect."

At this point, we are in a position to be able to "test and approve what God's will is." It all seems pretty simple and straightforward as we look at the progression in the passage. So, what is the problem? Why is it often so hard for us to come to a place of peace about what God's will is in our life situations?

Sometimes it just takes time and patience as we wait for this guidance. But other times, we are not at peace because we want to stay in control.

This is what can happen: We say, "God, please show me your will." But we have in mind very clearly what we want his will to be. For example: "God, please show me your will about whether I should marry Joe." We say the right words, but we have already determined in our hearts that this is what we want to do—that is, marry Joe.

It is like putting "blinders" on and facing in the direction of the answer we want. The reason that handlers put blinders on horses is to reduce distraction and keep them focusing straight ahead.

So with our blinders on, we say the right thing, but we do not allow ourselves to have peripheral vision. God may be bringing us something to look at that is coming from the left or the right, but we never see it; we are never "distracted" by it. After "praying" several times and seeing only what we want to see, we say, "I asked God and sought his will, and it is clear to me that I should marry Joe." But we never even took our blinders off.

It takes great faith to seek God's will with a submissive and surrendered spirit. The next time we are testing and approving, let's make sure to take our blinders off. Only then will our heart truly know the peace that passes all understanding.

32

Shrink the Giant Dot

Think of a time when you were totally overwhelmed. As you looked at your life, you saw it as completely unmanageable. You were stressed and could not imagine how in the world everything would work out. Maybe the pressure came from an assignment that was due in school or at work. Or a schedule that called for you to be three places at once. Or a house that was in total chaos and needed to be ready to receive visitors in a short time.

Remember what this felt like? What was happening was not in any way catastrophic, but it felt like it was. Even though that day was just a dot on a line representing your whole life, the dot was gigantic and all consuming. It blocked the view of everything else.

I flash back to a time twenty years ago. Our church was having a special women's event with 5000 women expected. I was in charge of the ushering for the three-day event and was down to the wire in getting the ushers' packets ready. For some now-forgotten reason, I was not able to get the packet ready in time to make copies. I was feeling incredibly overwhelmed and was, I am sure, freaking out as I thought of failing in this assignment.

Talk about one small dot seeming gigantic—this dot was Earth-sized to me at the time. I felt totally stymied and unable to finish this task.

Tom stepped in to rescue me. He went to the church office to make all the copies, stapled them and even made an attractive cover sheet. I was so relieved when he came home with that stack of packets.

Until right now, though, I had not thought of that day in years. My point is that what was so gargantuan to me then, is now only a tiny dot on the long line of my life.

More recently, as the managing editor of DPI, a Christian publishing company, I had prepared an e-mail marketing piece to send out to 8000 people. I double-checked it to make sure all was in order and sent it out. It wasn't long before several people responded: "Did you know you put '*Clam* My Anxious Heart' instead of '*Calm* My Anxious Heart' for that book title?" At first my "anxious heart" felt a bit "clammed." But then I had to laugh. "Clam My Anxious Heart" *is* funny.

I guess I have learned some about the "dot" principle. This mistake was a tiny dot—a tiny, funny dot on the line of my life.

In situations like this and many others, I try to remind myself to get perspective, to back up and see the whole line and realize that this day will take its proper place as a small dot when life moves on to the next day. What seems earth-shattering today will diminish in its stress-power by tomorrow, and even more by next month, next year, or ten years from now.

Maybe this is why God reminds us to "be still, and know that I am God" (Psalm 46:10). Maybe he wants us to remember what is ultimately important and to be at peace. This was what Paul was communicating to the church at Thessalonica:

> Now may the Lord of peace himself give you peace at all times and in every way. The Lord be with all of you. (2 Thessalonians 3:16)

Peace "at all times" (even when we are stressed and tempted to despair). Peace "in every way" (physically, mentally and spiritually). No matter the century nor the situation, we all need to keep perspective by taking a deep breath and looking to the Prince of Peace. He will help us to shrink the giant dots in our lives.

33

Sink or Swim

To the Jews who had believed him, Jesus said, "If you hold to my teaching, you are really my disciples. Then you will know the truth, and the truth will set you free."

John 8:31–32

This is a passage that is familiar to many of us. I want to share an analogy that has given it a deeper meaning in my life.

Imagine someone drowning in the deep end of a swimming pool. She falls in and never had swimming lesson one. In her distress she is calling to someone for help. This person urgently reaches for a life preserver tied to a rope and throws it out to her.

How does the drowning person respond to the presence of the flotation ring? Does she casually reach out for it, push it away from her, and then pull it back? Does she play around with it? No, she is desperate. She is drowning. She has no other possibility for saving her life. With every fiber of her being, she holds on. Every muscle is tensed. She knows this is her only chance of survival. She is not even tempted with being distracted or self-reliant.

So it is when we are given God's word in our life. Each one of us is that drowning person. We are all desperate for his word to save us and to give us life. We have no chance without it. The question is, "How serious and focused are we when it comes to holding to this truth?"

If we don't particularly like the truth that God's word is showing us, do we, as drowning people, start looking around for another life preserver? Do we say, "I don't like this red one; I want the blue one that is down at the end of the pool. Throw that one to me"? Do we become choosy? Do we become the judge of what is and what isn't truth?

God calls us to respect and to revere his words, his truth and his Son who embodies both. There is no place for casualness and comparison shopping. It is only when we accept his truth and hold on to it that we are his disciples, and this will set us free.

> Do not merely listen to the word, and so deceive yourselves. Do what it says. Anyone who listens to the word but does not do what it says is like a man who looks at his face in a mirror and, after looking at him-

self, goes away and immediately forgets what he looks like. But the man who looks intently into the perfect law that gives freedom, and continues to do this, not forgetting what he has heard, but doing it—he will be blessed in what he does. (James 1:22–25)

34

A Healthy Respect for I-65

Tom and I are on Interstate 65 many times during the week. Our church meets forty-five minutes away; our doctors' offices are thirty minutes away; downtown Nashville is forty minutes away. Going to all these places involves traveling on I-65.

Sometimes as I am mindlessly driving along on cruise control, I remind myself, "Don't take I-65 for granted. It is to be respected." I don't want to be fooled into thinking that I am in some kind of protective tunnel that will take me from my driveway to my destination with no danger as I travel up and down the familiar path of I-65.

It is easy to be lulled into a sense of safety, to be tricked into a casual mindset…only to be confronted by unexpected perils on the journey.

I tell myself to stay alert, to keep my eyes on the road, and not to fool around with the radio or my cell phone while going seventy miles an hour. The slightest swerve by me or a vehicle in front of me could send my car crashing out of control.

Now, mind you, I don't want to live in constant fear that tragedy is about to happen. An anxious driver is not a safe driver, so anxiety defeats the point of being safety conscious. But I do want to have a healthy respect for I-65. I think you get my point.

In the same way, we as Christians have routines every day and interact with many of the same people every day. Do we forget that we need to stay close to God so that we can respond the way he would want us to? Or since the territory is so familiar, do we just wing it, putting our actions into "cruise control"? Do we think we are doing great on our own as we go about our day? Do we realize that Satan is a roaring lion, seeking to devour us?

> Be self-controlled and alert. Your enemy the devil prowls around like a roaring lion looking for someone to devour. (1 Peter 5:8)

If we are distracted by all the goings-on around us and if we are just expecting that everything will be as it always is, we can get numb to our desperate need to rely upon God. We can get lulled into a sense of safety. We can be tricked into a casual mindset...only to be confronted by unexpected perils on the journey: a coworker whom we find attractive, a husband who is not feeling respected, a driver who cuts us off, a child who pushes all our buttons.

If we have the proper respect for life and for Satan's traps, we will prepare ourselves for the day. We will take on the fruit of the Spirit (Galatians 5:22–25) and put on the armor of God (Ephesians 6:11–18) before sallying forth into our day. Jesus told us that "each day has…trouble of its own" (Matthew 6:34). And you never know when you are going to run into that trouble.

As we drive, let's realize the danger, and respect the highways that we travel. And as we start each day, let's respect the life we live…and look to God to prepare us and protect us.

35

Spiritual Mazes

Your word is a lamp to my feet
and a light for my path.
Psalm 119:105

Do you ever feel out of touch with your faith? Do you get concerned that you can't seem to grasp biblical truths... you feel spiritually disconnected or out of it?

I do.

And when I do, I sometimes think, "What is the matter with me? Have I been a Christian all these years just to lose touch and not be able to hold on to my faith?"

Recently was such a time of spiritual disconnection for me. I was not into gross violations of my faith. No new sin had insinuated itself into my life. I was going through my days doing many of the right things. But I missed having that edge for God, that clear vision of my purpose, that deep sense of direction and comfort and conviction.

When I am in these spiritual doldrums, I find myself not

knowing exactly what to do to get out. Then God in some way reminds me that I cannot find my own way out of this maze, that he will guide me.

I remember going to an amusement park with a friend of mine. We went into a maze of mirrors. About halfway through, I felt a little frustrated and trapped. How could I get out of there? I had no clear path. I could not rely upon my great navigational skills. Everywhere I looked, I could not tell what was real and what was reflection.

So, I just kept on walking and seeking, and before long, I saw daylight—real daylight coming through an opening. I followed the light and stepped outside…very relieved.

While outside, I could see my friend still in the maze, trying to find her way out. Unfortunately, I found it funny to watch her trying fake passageway after passageway until she too finally emerged. To her it really was not funny. I am sure she was feeling the same frustration and low-grade panic that I had felt.

When I have lost my way spiritually and I am having trouble determining what is real and what is a mirrored reflection, I know that I cannot trust my own instincts. I can only trust God, who sees the way clearly, to show me. What I need to do is humbly come to him, admit my spiritual poverty, and ask for help.

What Paul says in 1 Corinthians 2 encourages me tremendously:

> However, as it is written:
>
> > "No eye has seen,
> >   no ear has heard,
> > no mind has conceived
> >   what God has prepared for those
> >   who love him"—
>
> but God has revealed it to us by his Spirit.
>   The Spirit searches all things, even the deep things of God. For who among men knows the thoughts of a man except the man's spirit within him? In the same way no one knows the thoughts of God except the Spirit of God. We have not received the spirit of the world but the Spirit who is from God, that we may understand what God has freely given us. This is what we speak, not in words taught us by human wisdom but in words taught by the Spirit, expressing spiritual truths in spiritual words.
>   (1 Corinthians 2:9–13)

I cannot discern spiritual truths by myself; I need God's Spirit. If I have not been spending deep time with God in his word and in prayer, my spiritual discernment is weakened. I can get frustrated and trapped. This passage says that as Christians we are given the Spirit "that we may understand what God has freely given us."

When I feel spiritually adrift, I am not understanding what God has freely given me. It is not time to rely upon myself to "figure out" how to get out of where I am. It is time to come before God, to ask for his help and to accept that even in my weakness, his Spirit will work in me to restore me.

It is my prayer that we will not continue to bump our heads on deceptive mirrors, feeling trapped in a spiritual maze. But, that instead, we will humbly look to God for his direction to guide us back to the light.

36

The Grace of Giving

He who did not spare his own Son, but gave him up for us all—how will he not also, along with him, graciously give us all things?

Romans 8:32

God is a giver. In fact, God is *the* giver: "For God so loved the world that he gave…" and he gave and he gave…and he keeps on giving.

To be like God, we must have givers' hearts. But have you noticed that such a heart does not come naturally? At least it doesn't come naturally for me.

It is my desire to "excel in this grace of giving" (2 Corinthians 8:7), to have a heart like God in this area. But sometimes I see another attitude at work in me. I find that there can be motives other than to participate in the nature of God. I find that my giving can be tainted with self-centered desires.

I can give because I have to, or I feel that I have to. It is expected of me. It is the right thing to do. It is what a Christian should do. This kind of giving is nothing more than legalism—following the letter of the law to make sure I am okay with God. It lacks the joy that the Spirit within wants to bring me.

Then I can give because I want people to see how giving I am. I want the praise of men instead of the praise of God. Jesus was clear about the fact that the praise of others is the only reward we get when this is our motive. We don't get the reward of joy in our hearts that comes simply from being like God (Matthew 6:4).

One other reason I can find lurking in my heart is the desire to be affirmed—for others to tell me that I am a good person. I want someone to notice me and think I am important or that I am spiritual. Instead of God and his affirmation being enough, I can say, "Words of affirmation are my love language—so affirm me when I give to someone." Ouch!

I am grateful that God shows me my heart, that he exposes my motives, and that he forgives and cleanses and restores me so I can know the true joy of giving. And what a joy this is!

I can be "cheerful" (2 Corinthians 9:7). I can be "gracious" (Romans 8:32). I can do my giving acts "in secret" and know God's reward that satisfies down deep in my soul (Matthew 6:1–4).

❄

While on this earth, these false motives will want to imperceptibly slide into our hearts and try to take up residence. But thank God that he searches our hearts:

> The lamp of the LORD searches the spirit
>   of a man;
>   it searches out his inmost being.
> (Proverbs 20:27)

Thank God that he keeps modeling for us the act of giving and that he keeps forgiving us and filling us with his Spirit. He takes our imperfect giving, and because we want to be like him, he encourages others through us.

Thank you, Jesus, for showing us that "it is more blessed to give than to receive" (Acts 20:35).

37

No Trespassing: Forbidden Territory

I remember a Christian sister coming to my house one night because she needed to talk to me. I didn't know her well and didn't know what was on her mind. It turned out that she had developed a negative attitude toward me. She assured me that I had not done anything to her, and the thoughts and feelings she had were not in response to any action on my part.

I breathed a sigh of relief there; I am sure you know what I mean. At least I was not about to get corrected for something I had done or said to her!

Then she went on to tell me that when she saw me teaching or leading, she would think, "I can do that!" Her sins were the evil twins of pride and jealousy, and they had polluted her heart toward me.

I was certainly understanding because those two had certainly come calling in my own life. In fact, they even lodged with me at times. I assured her of my forgiveness, and after some more talk and prayer, we ended the night together.

I went to bed feeling only forgiveness.

But...the next morning I got up and thought back over the events and the confession of the night before, and I began to think: "She thought *what*? She felt *what* toward me? I didn't do anything to her. I was just trying to be faithful to God. I can't believe she had such negative feelings toward me!"

Then came the reminder from God: "You forgave her."

An analogy came to me.

Have you ever been out in the countryside, hiking or walking or just enjoying the view, and you saw a sign that said clearly: "NO TRESPASSING"? That meant the land beyond that sign was forbidden territory. You should not set foot upon it.

In the same way, when we forgive someone, God puts up a no-trespassing sign. Forbidden territory. We should not set foot upon it. Once we have forgiven, we can't "take it back" as if our fingers were crossed.

To forgive is a sacred action—one motivated, sanctioned

and sealed by the Holy Spirit. No tromping around on that land any more.

When thoughts of wanting to reconsider forgiveness come up, we need to remind ourselves—no trespassing. The deed is done. We need to forgive as God has forgiven us.

> In him we have redemption through his blood, the forgiveness of sins, in accordance with the riches of God's grace that he lavished on us with all wisdom and understanding. (Ephesians 1:7–8)

> "And when you stand praying, if you hold anything against anyone, forgive him, so that your Father in heaven may forgive you your sins." (Mark 11:25)

38

The Winter of Our Content

The other day I was driving back from Alabama into Tennessee, my new home—my new green home. During spring and summer, I typically comment, "I love the green." And I do. For a green lover, there is no better place to be than Middle Tennessee with its verdant meadows, hills and valleys.

As I was surveying the undulating landscape surrounding I-65, I found myself feeling a bit sad and even a bit put out that winter was sneaking in to steal my green. I saw the signs of it: the trees, not quite in fall plumage, were tinged with an ochre weariness. The shorter days were conspiring to drain the leaves of green and to ultimately consign them, dead and shriveled, to the ground.

Of course, I told myself it was silly to have an attitude toward winter, but that really didn't change my mind. So, I thought, I am going to have to come up with a whole new paradigm, an entirely different way of looking at this situation. I need to see winter through the eyes of contentment. Didn't Paul say, "I have learned to be content in any situation, whether in summer or winter, whether in green or gray" (or something to that effect)?

So I searched for some thoughts to rival those negative ones in my mind:

(1) See the beauty in all seasons. See the different stages of life in the trees, and marvel at the buds and baby leaves in spring. At the seemingly infinite shades of green in the summer. At the resplendent regalia of autumn, and at the stark beauty of the trees' nakedness in winter, silhouetted against a slate gray sky. There is glory in each stage of life because God is in it.

> There is a time for everything,
> and a season for every activity under
> heaven. (Ecclesiastes 3:1)

(2) Just as the trees drop their dead leaves and then experience the new birth of green leaves in the spring, so we must die to ourselves to experience new birth. And resurrection is a sure thing—spiritually and physically. God displays such a profound analogy to illustrate our own new birth.

> Praise be to the God and Father of our Lord Jesus

Christ! In his great mercy he has given us new birth
into a living hope through the resurrection of Jesus
Christ from the dead. (1 Peter 1:3)

(3) More than anything, let the constancy of the seasons
remind us of God's constancy:

"As long as the earth endures,
seedtime and harvest,
cold and heat,
summer and winter,
day and night
will never cease." (Genesis 8:22)

"Let us acknowledge the LORD;
  let us press on to acknowledge him.
As surely as the sun rises,
  he will appear;
he will come to us like the winter rains,
  like the spring rains that water the earth."
(Hosea 6:3)

(4) Snow even speaks of God.

Showing his involvement in our weather and our world:

He spreads the snow like wool
  and scatters the frost like ashes.
(Psalm 147:16)

Reminding us of our total forgiveness, no matter how
grievous our sin:

> Cleanse me with hyssop, and I will be clean;
>   wash me, and I will be whiter than snow.
> (Psalm 51:7)

So, going into the winter, I am choosing to have a different mind set—not to feel like the victim of a verdant robbery, but to be reminded of an artistic, loving, accepting and constant Father who speaks to me daily through his varied handiwork.

39

Live in Harmony

Finally, all of you, live in harmony with one another;
be sympathetic, love as brothers, be compassionate
and humble. Do not repay evil with evil or insult with
insult, but with blessing, because to this you were
called so that you may inherit a blessing.

1 Peter 3:8–9

The fiery, impassioned, unpredictable Peter learned from
his master. He became a submissive man who was in tune
with the movement of the newly sent Holy Spirit within
him. The prompting and stirring of that divine Spirit is
seen through the pages of his letter that we now call First
Peter.

It is his heart's concern that we "show proper respect to
everyone" and "love the brotherhood of believers" (2:17).
Then in verses 8 and 9 (above) he sums up his thoughts
by appealing to the brothers and sisters to "live in harmony with one another."

I am not by any means a musical expert, but I understand

the concept of musical chords. Each chord is comprised of a number of notes that when played at the same time, elicit a pleasant sound that is referred to as "harmony." Two notes can harmonize, three notes can harmonize, and more than three can harmonize.

If you play a note that is not part of the chord, what you get is dissonance, which is a "harsh or disagreeable combination of sounds." You get "discord," and it is unpleasant to your ears.

When Peter's counterpart, Paul, writes in Galatians 5, he tells us that discord is an act of the sinful nature, not a work of the Spirit.[1] I see a discordant person as one who knows the right "note" to play, but purposefully plays the wrong one. She knows how God would have her respond, but she does not choose to respond this way. She is not seeking unity with others, but is rather seeking to please herself.

Now understand that I am not advocating "people pleasing" here. I don't mean that you try to figure out what note someone wants you to play in order to harmonize with him or her, and then you play that note no matter what your own conviction is.

---

1. The Greek word *eris* ("discord" in NIV) means "contention, debate, strife, variance" (Galatians 5:20).

What I mean is you should strive to play the note that God wants you to play in any given situation or relationship. Then, as others are also playing the note God wants them to play, the couple or group or friends will experience a harmony conducted by the Holy Spirit himself.

I know at times I have been a discordant person. I have played the wrong note simply because I was too prideful or too stubborn to play the right one. In such times, I have stood in need of God's grace and the grace of the other "note players" in my life.

Have you noticed that if you just play one note, there is no possibility of either harmony or discord? It is when you bring notes together that one or the other will exist. And life is full of many notes, many relationships, many opportunities to interact with others.

Think about the different relationships you are in. Then ask yourself about each of them: "Am I being harmonious or discordant?" Let's pray that God will give us the right notes and help us have humble hearts that are eager to play them.

40

A Child of the Wind

"The wind blows wherever it pleases. You hear its sound, but you cannot tell where it comes from or where it is going. So it is with everyone born of the Spirit."

John 3:8

When I was a young adult, I used to write poetry. It was helpful and satisfying to capture thoughts that flowed with clarity, cadence and simplicity. I even tried to find a publisher who would pay attention to my manuscript…but to no avail. Now a publisher myself, I can identify with those who receive the dreaded "rejection letters" (or actually, e-mails) from me.

I still have my poems and go back and read them every once in a while. Sometimes a snippet from one will come to me…lines such as

> Let me bow,
> Let me bend.
> Let me be, like the trees,
> a child of the wind.

When I was in college, I remember once sitting in my friend's dorm room, looking out the window at twilight. As I watched the trees blowing and tossing in the wind, I was certainly thinking of Jesus' words comparing the movement of the Spirit to the movement of the wind. Though you can see neither, you can experience the results of both.

The Greek word for "spirit" is the same as the one for "wind": *pneuma*. It can also mean "breath," and each, in its way, is the very breath of God.

It is mesmerizing to witness the graceful, yielding dance of the trees, sensitive to the slightest movement of the wind. It is only the stubborn, stiff and sapless ones who refuse to bow and to bend. These are the ones who are destroyed and gathered up in pieces after the storm passes by.

The supple, submissive ones are God's visual aid, inviting us to join the dance...to become, like the trees, a child of the wind:

What does it mean in your life to be submissive to God, to "keep in step with the [dance of the] Spirit"? (See Galatians 5:25.) Does it mean being patient in a frustrating work situation? Being kind in a challenging family relationship? Being flexible when life is not predictable and is a bit upside down? Being obedient when God calls you to change something in your character? Or being selfless when everything in you wants to shout, "What about me?"

Remember the message of the swaying trees, and allow yourself to bow and bend with the blowing of God's Spirit in your life.

Thoughts from the Author

In this first part of *My Bucket of Sand,* it has been my joy to share my heart with you. You likely will not be able to build sand castles with what you read, but hopefully you gained some helpful insights. It is very satisfying to be able to write out thoughts and understandings that, sometimes, I have had for years.

If anything in this book was beneficial or valuable to you, I encourage you to share it with someone else. Now that you have the thought, it's in your bucket too.

I see this book as a legacy of sorts, a bequest to my children (both physical and spiritual). And it is a great reminder to all of us to write down and pass on what we have learned along the way. Those who come after us will be grateful that we did.

Thank you for joining me. It is my prayer that God will give us strength to persevere to the end, no matter what life brings to each of us. In his grace…

Other Writings

The following five chapters are ones I wrote for various anthologies published by DPI. I offer these as added resources for your encouragement. Since these chapters were written several years ago, some of the personal facts are out of date. Some chapters are addressed to everyone, while others are addressed to single women, to wives or to mothers. I encourage everyone to read the chapter addressed to single women because the information in it is helpful to all women.

Who Gets the Credit?
Thirty Days at the Foot of the Cross

> May I never boast except in the cross of our Lord Jesus
> Christ, through which the world has been crucified to me,
> and I to the world.
> Galatians 6:14

"I did it all by myself." The boast of a two-year-old who has just put his shoes on for the first time? No, the thought of a thirty-two-year-old who has just completed a marathon. Or of a twenty-seven-year-old who has just received the Employee of the Month Award. How quick human nature is to accept credit for certain accomplishments. How quick human nature is to forget that God made us and enables us to run, to think, to breathe. Paul asks us, *"What do you have that you did not receive? And if you did receive it, why do you boast as if you did not?"* (1 Corinthians 4:7b).

We like to feel strong, to feel adequate, to feel talented. It builds our self-esteem. It verifies our worth. And so we look for reasons to boast. Of course, we often don't recognize it as boasting. We don't see the arrogance in our hearts as we self-sufficiently go into our day without prayer. We are, in effect, saying, "I can do it all by myself." We are saying, *"Today... [I] will go to this or that city..."* (James 4:13). James says we are boasting and bragging.

Do we think that Paul had low self-esteem because he said, *"I will not boast about myself, except about my weaknesses."* (2 Corinthians 12:5b)? Does low self-esteem motivate someone to

145

be the selfless, compassionate, pivotal leader of a persecuted, fledgling movement? Boast in our weaknesses? It is upside down. It is inside out. And yet, it is true—through and through. Paul's commitment was clear. *"May I never boast except in the cross of our Lord Jesus Christ."* The cross affirms our worth. The cross frees us from performing, from making sure we get the credit due us. In our old natures, we take that credit and very carefully wrap our sense of worth around it. We are fearful of losing any credit, because that would lessen the amount of worth that we could wrap around it. Less credit—less worth, we reason.

Why was Paul willing to boast about his weaknesses? He lets us in on the secret—*"I will boast all the more gladly about my weaknesses, so that Christ's power may rest on me.... For when I am weak, then I am strong"* (2 Corinthians 12:9b, 10b). Who would not want the power of God in his life? The power that created a universe out of nothing. The power that parted the Red Sea. The power that raised a very dead man from the grave never to die again. Who wouldn't want it? But how does Paul say you can have that power? By boasting in your weaknesses. By not making sure you get credit for all your strengths. Upside down. Inside out. But true—through and through.

So, how do we respond to this? Do we snivel around saying, "I'm so weak. I can't do anything. I'm no good to anybody"? Remember what Paul said, *"When I am weak, then I am*

strong." The person who truly boasts in the cross and in what Jesus has done for her is a strong person. A person who does not rely on recognition from others to stay faithful to God. A person who does not pull away from others if they do not seem to appreciate her enough. Yes, a strong person. A person who can take correction without having to prove all the ways she *is* right. A person who is secure enough in her own worth that she can tell the truth to someone who might reject her. A person who does not have to prove she already knew something before she was told. Bottom line—a person who can admit her inadequacies and confess her sins and look to God for verification. One who is free of the need to project an image or prove her worth. And one through whom the power of God is able to flow unhindered. Such a person is not boastful, but is humble. Such a person is strong, is spiritual and puts her trust in God. Are you such a person? Do you want to be such a person?

In my old nature I look to be affirmed, to be given credit for all that I do. I naturally try to prove that I am worthy of others' love and respect. A competitive spirit, a self-oozing instead of self-losing spirit spits out of my heart apart from Jesus.

At times, I have been publicly affirmed for something I really did not do. Certain traits were ascribed to me that I personally did not see. On the other hand, my name has also been left out of the "list of credits" for things I played a major role in accomplishing. A little voice comes up in me that wants to set the record straight on both counts. But the cross says that the record has already been set straight. All credit to Jesus. So be it.

Thanks be to God that Jesus has taken the credit for my prideful heart and that he has given me credit for his righteousness. This is the reckoning miracle of the cross. Therefore, all credit for my own righteousness is his.

As you look at your own heart, are you boastful or are you humble? Do you trust in yourself and your own abilities, or do you trust in God? Do you acknowledge that your talents are gifts from God, or do you feel better than others in the areas of your strengths? Are you trying to earn your salvation, or are you grateful that Jesus has already won it? Do you push others away in your need to prove yourself, or do you draw others to you through your vulnerability?

Boast in your weaknesses. Live in the power of God. It is upside down. It is inside out. But it is true—through and through.

For further study:
Deuteronomy 8:10–18; Daniel 4:28–37; Romans 4;
2 Corinthians 2:1–5, 5:11–21.

Thomas A. Jones and Sheila Jones, eds. *Thirty Days at the Foot of the Cross* (Spring Hill, TN: DPI, 1993).

Elizabeth: A Childlike Heart
She Shall Be Called Woman Volume 2

Being a priest of God was an honor. You could not buy it or earn it. You were simply born to it—you had to be a descendant of Aaron. Certain restrictions were placed on priests, especially when it came to marriage.

A priest had to marry a virgin who was not the daughter of a former slave. She also had to be a true Jew, not a proselyte. If a priest were widowed without children, he could not marry a woman who was "incapable." In addition to these restrictions, the high priest had to marry a woman who also belonged to a priestly family.

What a difficult situation it must have been for the barren wife of a priest. But the God who parted the Red Sea delights in changing difficult situations. (Reading—Luke 1:1–80)

She glanced at the familiar shadow of the tree behind their house. Calculating the position of the sun, she knew it was around 4:00 in the afternoon. Her husband should be home soon since the walk from Jerusalem took the better part of a day. She wiped her hands on a nearby cloth, glancing absently at the age spots that had begun to show in the last year. She shook the flour from her garment and placed the freshly baked bread on the table. Knowing he would be tired and hungry, she wanted the meal to be ready when he returned.

Walking out the door, she shaded her eyes against the slanted rays of the sun and strained to see down the road. A few carts passed and several small groups of laborers. Finally she saw him—a familiar figure in the distance. His determined, head-down, no-nonsense gait always notified her of his approach. Although he was beginning to show signs of aging, he was still a strong man with a confident stride.

As he came closer, she began to feel a certain uneasiness. What was the matter? When he was close enough for her to clearly see his features, she saw a look on his face she had never seen before—not in all their years of married life. Elizabeth, an older woman herself, had known her share of tragedy. She braced herself for whatever news he was bringing. But she could never have prepared herself for the incredible happening he would soon share with her. As he stood before her, silent and moving his hands wildly, she would soon understand that what she had misread as tragedy was really the most wonderful news she would ever receive.

The Visitation

What frustration Zechariah must have felt as he tried to communicate to his bewildered wife what had happened to him a few days earlier at the temple. As a priest, a descendant of Aaron, he served with his division one week out of every six. He had been assigned by lot the duty of offering the incense—first thing each morning and last thing each night. While he was on duty, an angel appeared to him—not an everyday occurrence, even for a priest! Uneasy and fearful, Zechariah stared dumbfounded. The angel comforted him and brought him a message of hope, of answered prayer, of a son who would lead the people back to God.

Unfortunately, Zechariah allowed his amazement to give birth to a sinful attitude. Standing before the messenger of the God of Abraham, Isaac and Jacob, he displayed a "show me" attitude. In the annals of Hebrew history, others had questioned God and were simply answered. How did he *sin* in his questioning? In *unbelief.* The angel said, "And now you will be silent and not able to speak until the day this happens, because you did not believe my words" (Luke 1:20). Unbelief spawns arrogance, cynicism and ingratitude. In the presence of *the* sign, his intellect cried out for *a* sign. As a result, he was disciplined by the Most High God as he stood in *his* temple before *his* altar and *his* messenger. God's reproof came swiftly. No *ifs.* No *ands.* No *buts.* Punctuated by the statement, "I am Gabriel. I stand in the presence of God" (Luke 1:19).

Zechariah must have re-entered the courtyard a changed man. Totally humbled, totally repentant and totally convinced. A righteous man was being purified to receive and raise a messenger for God.

The Wait

Zechariah and Elizabeth are described as "upright in the sight of God" (Luke 1:6). They were devout and sincere—both descendants of Aaron. He, a priest; she, the daughter of a priest. The fact that she also was from a priestly family would have added to their already respected position in the community.

What must Elizabeth have felt as her husband laboriously communicated to her without words the incredible news he had received? Her mind must have flashed back to memories of her father telling her about Abraham and Sarah, about the astounding news they too received from a messenger of God. Sarah had laughed to think of having a child—and yet, Elizabeth's faith had the benefit of knowing what had happened to Sarah. She *did* have a child in her old age, and that child became the father of Israel, Elizabeth's nation. How foolish it would be for her not to believe. God had once again chosen to work his will in the body of one who was "well along in years." Miracle of miracles! *She* was to have a baby!

What wonder, as she experienced the first stirrings of life within. The breasts that had sagged with age were now full and round, preparing to nurse the child she had thought she would never have. For decades she had rejoiced with and comforted pregnant friends. She had listened to their good-natured complaints of kicks in the ribs, of bladders urgent with the pressure of an enlarging uterus, of the elasticity of skin stretched as never before. Now, wonder of wonders, it was happening to her!

Even in the excitement and wonder of it all, she could not help but feel some fear, some sense of the strangeness of it all. This body she had known and cared for over the years had never done things it was doing now. She probably felt somewhat out of control, but then she would surely remember that the gift was from God, and he would bring that gift to term and deliver it. In all the wonder, strangeness and lack of control, she was filled with inexplicable joy. After years of prayer and hope, she had totally given up. Her ovaries had shriveled, her tubes had long since ceased to carry eggs to be fertilized. New life from the author of life. Something from nothing—the paradox of his nature.

The Visit

While Elizabeth was in her sixth month of pregnancy, the angel, Gabriel, made another visit—this time to her young relative, Mary of Nazareth. The news brought to Mary was even more incredible. She was a virgin and was to become pregnant without sexual union with a man. She was to bear God's Son—the Savior of his people.

Hearing that Elizabeth was also experiencing a miraculous pregnancy, Mary hurried to the hill country to visit her relative. What a joy for Elizabeth! With so many new things happening in her body, her heart, her soul, she longed to talk with her husband as she once had—when he was able to speak. The most incredible event was happening, and they could not speak of it together. With Mary there, she finally had someone with whom she could share her heart. Someone who would truly understand. Someone who was also bearing a miracle of God.

Zechariah must have struggled as he looked at his wife's expanding figure with awe and wonder—to sleep next to an unfolding miracle and not be able to praise God aloud was a discipline that would have grown more difficult each day. Yet, because of his devout heart before God, we can imagine that Zechariah did not harbor resentment toward a righteous God who disciplined only for his own good. God must have been preparing his faith so he could father a child who would grow to be a unique and powerful man of God.

As Mary first approached Elizabeth, the child in Elizabeth's womb kicked with exhilaration and anticipation in the presence of *Emmanuel*—"God with us"—in embryonic form. He had come to her, and she was honored beyond belief as the Spirit filled her:

> "Blessed are you among women and blessed is the child you will bear! But why am I so favored, that the mother of my Lord should come to me? As soon as the sound of your greeting reached my ears, the baby in my womb leaped for joy. Blessed is she who has believed that what the Lord has said to her will be accomplished" (Luke 1:42–45).

She spoke words from God himself; she was the first to announce the coming of the Messiah. The fruit of the Spirit within her was humility; she gladly accepted that the son of the older would serve and prepare the way for the son of the younger. There was no sign of pride, of competitiveness. If God wanted to work through a younger woman, then let it be. A humble mother would give birth to a humble son. In years to come, he also would be honored that Emmanuel came to him in the form of his younger cousin: "But one more powerful than I will come, the thongs of whose sandals I am not worthy to untie" (Luke 3:16).

It should be no surprise that Mary stayed for three months. Not only was she probably experiencing morning sickness, but she and Elizabeth had much to share. They must have daily shook their heads in amazement and compared notes on their progressing pregnancies.

How they must have held on to each other when she *did* leave. They must have looked deeply into each other's eyes, satisfied with the sense of shared wonder and faith—two ordinary women in an ordinary house experiencing something supernaturally extraordinary. They were each bearing sons who would affect the world for eternity.

The Birth

First labor, even when your child has been miraculously conceived, is *still* first labor. Elizabeth experienced the process of birth from a different perspective that day. She had undoubtedly attended others during their times of delivery. Now she was the one being attended. One last triumphant push, adrenaline pumping, forehead sweating...out he came—hairy and yelling at the top of his lungs. John—to be called the Baptist— emerged from the watery sac of protection and announced to the world, *I am here.* The Spirit within announced to the heavenly realms, *God is here, and he is ready to unfold the plan of the ages.* The forerunner of the Messiah was cleaned, wrapped in clean cloths, and placed in the trembling arms of his mother. A son. So long she had waited. Too soon she had given up. What did God have in store for this miracle baby? *I must have the heart of Hannah. I must give him back to God—my Samuel, his chosen.*

On the eighth day when the neighbors came for the circumcision, they assumed that he would take his father's name. After all, he was the firstborn, and surely to be the *lastborn!* But his mother, with conviction, said, "No! He is to be called John" (Luke 1:60).

She must be out of her mind. Her pregnancy has made her mad. To their amazement, Zechariah wrote on the slate, "His name is John" (Luke 1:63). Immediately, his captive tongue was loosed. Through the Spirit, he poured out praise to God—praise stored up for ten long months in the heart of this new father of a prophet. The people marveled. The talk spread around the region. "What then is this child going to be?" (Luke 1:66).

Surely, Elizabeth, like Mary, pondered in her heart the words spoken by the angel concerning her son. She would see him "turn the hearts of the fathers to their children and the disobedient to the wisdom of the righteous—to make ready a people prepared for the Lord" (Luke 1:17).

The humble and powerful son of this humble and grateful mother would eventually be beheaded for boldly speaking the truth of God to a king—and was surely welcomed home by *the* King. God gave her a gift and she gave him back, and they were both blessed in the giving.

Can Good Be Bad?

Personal Response

A heart filled with the Holy Spirit is grateful. Vulnerable. Childlike. Unguarded. This is Elizabeth as she greeted Mary. She was filled with gratitude and awe that the mother of her Lord would come to her. I need to be like this woman.

Her grateful heart moved her to be unguarded. She did not allow protective defenses to go up. Like a two-year-old, this mature woman poured out her heart...loudly. This challenges me. When I personally share my thoughts and feelings, I want my responses to be pre-washed, neatly packaged and delivered. Very safe. Very protected. No risks.

I tend to be *good* by not saying what I am really thinking and feeling in situations. My good is really *bad*. My good is really dishonesty. It becomes a barrier to my relationship with everyone in my life, including God. And Jesus came to show us, and everyone else, who we really are—in order to change us into his image. It is silly to act like I already *am* what I am supposed to be. I want to be like Jesus, but that only happens when I stop *sanitizing* myself *by* myself. I must consistently be open about who I am. God already knows anyway. And others cannot help me change or give me the encouragement I need if I am not real with them.

Emotions still scare me. I guess sometimes I'm afraid I won't be able to control them. And I much prefer to feel in control. I don't like to deal with things in front of people. I am afraid of what might come out, of what might have been caged up. I prefer to take my "bone" to the corner, away from others, and "chew" on it. When I get to the level of my emotional discomfort, I feel like a little kid. I do not feel like a forty-six-year-old, mature mother, wife and editor. Precisely the need! "Unless you change and become like little children, you will never enter the kingdom of heaven" (Matthew 18:3). The fear of the unknown is strong. But he who is in me is stronger. Jesus did come to set us free. And it is only when we are free that we can truly bear the burdens of others on whatever level they need us.

I do not want honesty at the expense of sensitivity. I also do not want deceit under the guise of discernment. But I would rather make a mistake than build an image. I am never more alive than when I am vulnerable. It is only then that I realize how much I need discipling by others and by God.

Elizabeth did not hold back in sharing her heart with Mary. Her childlike spirit is a call to all of us to lay down our defenses and to open up our hearts. Don't let fear, competitiveness or insecurity keep you from being all God wants you to be. God *is* faithful. He will fulfill his promise to you and me—just as he fulfilled his promise to Elizabeth.

Focus Question:

Are you open or guarded in your relationships? Would you rather make a mistake and grow, or be unreal and build an image?

Linda Brumley and Sheila Jones, eds. *She Shall Be Called Woman, Vol 2, Second Edition, New Testament Women* (Spring Hill, TN: DPI, 1998). This book is available from DPI along with volume 1 (*Old Testament Women*).

Single Women and Sexuality
Life and Godliness for Everywoman: Volume 1

At the dawn of time, God brought into being the apex of his creative energies: man and woman. They were sexual beings, with distinctive components to identify *which* sex. Through the centuries, God continued to create in the wombs of mothers-to-be, men and women—sexual beings. He created you and me. Whether we are single or married, we are sexual beings.

Think about it: How often have you seen the words "single" and "sexual" used together without "sin" somehow being the unifying context? It is very important that we, as followers of Jesus, understand the need for single women to be "at home" and at peace with their sexuality. I address this chapter to my single sisters…younger, older and in-between.

Understand That You Are a Sexual Being

God created you to be a woman. He gazed at *you*, his creation, and he said with all the power and conviction that only the Almighty Creator can have, "It is good." You have certain characteristics that he designed that indicate clearly that you are a woman: breasts, a uterus, ovaries, a vagina.

You are the balance of the men that God also created as sexual beings. By balance I mean that God put you on this earth to make it softer, more beautiful, more gentle. Your curves soften the landscape of humanity. And that is true whether you are married or single.

Many single women are confused by their sexuality and afraid of it. They do not want to sin sexually, so they simply deny that they are sexual. They begin to take on an identity of being "asexual"—they think of themselves as having no sexuality. This seems safer. More spiritual. Less confusing. But what it really is, is weird. Out of touch. Dishonest. Unrelatable.

Can a single woman make peace with her sexuality? If she acknowledges its presence, will it hurt her? Will it lead her into sin? Will it coil up as the serpent in the garden and entice her down the path…and out of the garden?

Quite the opposite—embracing her sexuality will invite her to enjoy being the woman God made her to be. It will help her to give of her softness and gentleness to others. When she feels hormonal stirrings or bodily reactions to sexual stimuli, she will remind herself not to be surprised…because she is a sexual being. She will not overreact to these hormonal stirrings or bodily reactions. She will not recoil in grief or guilt. She will smile to herself and say, "Yes, I am a woman. This comes with the territory."

To get more specific…when she is in the middle of her monthly cycle, and very easily stimulated vaginally with the mere pressure of the seam of her jeans on her clitoris, she will realize that she has not sinned. That ability to have an involuntary response to stimulus is just part of her makeup as a woman. Of course, she then has a decision to make as to whether she will encourage that stimulation and fantasize and purposely bring herself to an orgasm…or…whether she will affirm to herself, "Yes, I am a woman and this is a natural response. If I didn't have this response, I wouldn't be a woman, and I am glad to be a woman. Now, I need to get about the rest of my day and give to people and serve my God. And I might need to take these jeans off and wear something less confining so I won't be so distracted today."

You see, that is a healthy response. She doesn't overreact. She doesn't wallow in guilt. She doesn't reason that she has already sinned anyway, she might as well enjoy it and go ahead and fantasize and masturbate or flirt with some guy around her. She is a woman, but she is a woman who makes decisions to keep herself pure. (We will talk more about purity and temptation later.)

Understanding Your Sexual Past

Single women come from many different sexual backgrounds when they become disciples. In making this most-important decision in their lives, they confess and repent of sexual sins and commit to sexual purity. They vow to be celibate until they marry, if marriage is in God's plan for their lives. After this, very little is mentioned to women about their sexuality and how to deal with it practically—except when they are asked by those close to them, "Are you being sexually pure?"

With each type of background come specific thoughts about men, about dating and about sexuality:

1. If you have been with many men sexually in the past, you might have measured your worth by whom you

attract and how long you keep him. You may feel insecure as a person, and certainly as a woman, because you
do not currently "have a man." You may feel an inner
drive to prove or to affirm your femininity by being on
the arm of a guy you can call your own…whether he is
a disciple or not.

2. If you have had some relationships with men in the past
   that were satisfying not only sexually, but also emotionally, you will miss the intimacy of those relationships.
   You may feel incomplete in some ways because you are
   no longer sharing your life, your body, your bed with a
   man. You may think that you could not be in a pure
   relationship with a Christian man, so you hide behind
   some extra weight you have gained. You decide that if
   you ever do have a boyfriend, he will have to be someone you are not necessarily attracted to because you are
   afraid you will not be able to be pure otherwise.

3. If you have never had a sexual relationship with a man
   because of convictions from your upbringing or because
   of your own fears, you could wonder what it is like to be
   with a man. Your thoughts and current fears are somewhat different from those of Woman #1 and Woman #2
   above. You could be tempted, after several years as a con-
   tinuing-to-be-celibate single, to want to be "in the know"
   about this sexual relationship stuff. You can feel that you
   are the only "uninitiated" person around, and you can
   toy with giving away your virginity.

4. If you have suffered abuse in the past at the hands of men in your life, you might have an aversion to sex. You might be thinking, "I'm glad I don't have to have anything to do with this whole thing ever again." The problem is, though, that you are not open to learning about the beauty of the sexual relationship as God planned it in marriage. On the other hand, you might have an addiction to sex because of the experiences you have gone through at an early age. You will need the help of those close to you to break the hold that sex has on you. Instead of using relationships in order to feel "in control," you will need to learn to let God be in control of your life. Then you will be able to have healthy, nonsexual relationships with men.

Certainly there are other backgrounds, but these four begin to give us an idea of all the different roads that converge in the waters of baptism. In each and every situation, you have to figuratively go back in time, and learn about God's view of sexuality, of men and women, of the sex act and of what it means to have a relationship with a man.

I remember a young single woman who became a disciple while she was pregnant. We took a walk together, and she said, "I feel like a junior high school kid again. I don't know how to date or what to think about a relationship with a brother. It is very humbling." Indeed, entering the kingdom calls us to go through a very narrow door. We leave behind our old understandings, and we humbly learn and accept new ones.

Let's take a quick look at God's view of sex and the sexual relationship. It is quite different from that of the secular world's view and even of much of the religious world's view.

Accepting God's View of Sex

As we grew up, we had much curiosity and much confusion about sex. Think about the sources from which you learned your first tidbits of sexual information. It was usually from peers, from movies, from jokes…and seldom from parents or church leaders. Such mystery. Such interest. Such repulsion. Such childish understanding of a grown-up thing.

God wants us to have a mature understanding of his original plan. We, as disciples, have every reason to be open about sex since it was our Father's idea. The whole design of male and female and their complementary parts was his, not Satan's. We should have more relevant, more concise, more accurate understandings than anybody else. There is no shame in anything that God ordained. There is only shame in participating in Satan's distortion of what God ordained.

Some of the purposes of the sexual relationship in marriage are

- Procreation ("Be fruitful and multiply.")
- Pleasure (Song of Songs has explicit sexual description of the marriage relationship—also see Proverbs 5:18–19; Hebrews 13:4; 1 Corinthians 7.)
- Communication/Intimacy ("I give myself to you in a way that I give to no one else.")

- Health (relieves tension, burns calories, good for the heart—NOTE: God will still enable you to be healthy without sex in your life. I think he knew that the constant and intimate sharing of your life with someone could bring tension and strife, so sexual intimacy oils the relationship and keeps it moving smoothly when approached God's way. When not approached God's way, it can actually *bring* tension and strife.)
- Visual aid to the world and to the spiritual powers in the heavenly realms (Ephesians 5:22–23, tying in with Ephesians 3:10—shows God's oneness with his people. In the Old Testament, God=husband and Israel=wife.)

So, if sex is a good thing in God's eyes, why did so many of us grow up thinking it was dirty, bad, shameful? We can thank many of our ancestors for the distortion:

- Greek view of body and spirit—Gnosticism (or dualism) taught that the body is evil, and the spirit is good. Sex is of the body and is therefore evil.
- Augustine's teaching of "original sin"—Sin is passed on through the act of intercourse.
- Medieval Catholic theologians' distorted view—One theologian said that sex is so evil that the Holy Spirit got up and left the room when a married couple engaged in the sex act. It was viewed as a necessary evil to bring children into the world.
- Strict limitations on intercourse in the early years of the

Catholic church: During the week no sex was allowed on
- Thursday, out of respect for Christ's arrest;
- Friday, out of respect for Christ's death;
- Saturday, out of respect for Mary;
- Sunday, out of respect for Christ's resurrection;
- Monday, out of respect for the saints.

So, a married couple could only have sex on Tuesdays and Wednesdays without feeling guilty!

God created the sexual relationship and said that in marriage it is pure. Satan takes that good gift of God (as he does every good gift of God) and he twists it, drags it in the mud, uses it to hurt people, and laughs as he robs them of their purity. If we then react to the distortion and think that sex is dirty or shameful, we give Satan a double victory. As single women, you can say that a sexual relationship is good in the right context (marriage), but that you are not currently in that context…so for you a sexual relationship is not God's will. This is a healthy understanding and a healthy response to the gift and to the distortion.

Satan's Promises Vs. God's Promises

Imagine that a vacuum cleaner salesman comes to your door. His company has told him that he is free to make any claim he wants about what the product will do. There is no requirement for it to actually be able to do what he claims. So he makes some incredible promises to you: this machine will not only vacuum your floors, but it will also wash your dishes, make up your beds, wash your car and train your dog. *Amazing*, you think, and in your excitement you give him cash...much cash...to buy his ware.

The man leaves you with your wonder machine, but you soon find out that it can do none of the tasks he promised—in fact, it won't even vacuum your floors. The guy is gone with your money, and you are left to feel taken advantage of and ashamed of your gullibility.

In the same way, Satan is free to make any promise to you about what premarital sex will do for you: it will make you savvy and cool; it will give you fulfillment; it will bring intimacy; it will build your self-esteem; it will cause your man to be faithful to you for life. Yes, Satan can make any promises he wants, because his "company" doesn't require that the promises are true. In fact, he is a liar by nature. He makes his promises, takes your money, and leaves you to feel taken advantage of and ashamed of your gullibility.

Do not listen to the promises of Satan. Listen, instead, to the promises and the commands of God. He is the one who created you, who loves you, who wants the very best for you...whether you are married or single. And that very God says to you, as a single woman,

> "Food for the stomach and the stomach for food"—but God will destroy them both. The body is not meant for sexual immorality, but for the Lord, and the Lord for the body. (1 Corinthians 6:13)

> Flee from sexual immorality. All other sins a man commits

are outside his body, but he who sins sexually sins against his own body. (1 Corinthians 6:18)

But among you there must not be even a hint of sexual immorality, or of any kind of impurity, or of greed, because these are improper for God's holy people. (Ephesians 5:3)

Put to death, therefore, whatever belongs to your earthly nature: sexual immorality, impurity, lust, evil desires and greed, which is idolatry. (Colossians 3:5)

It is God's will that you should be sanctified: that you should avoid sexual immorality; that each of you should learn to control his own body in a way that is holy and honorable, not in passionate lust like the heathen, who do not know God; and that in this matter no one should wrong his brother or take advantage of him. The Lord will punish men for all such sins, as we have already told you and warned you. For God did not call us to be impure, but to live a holy life. Therefore, he who rejects this instruction does not reject man but God, who gives you his Holy Spirit. (1 Thessalonians 4:3–8)

It is never God's plan to discriminate against you. He does not like you less than married people, only giving this particular privilege to them. He wants what is best for you, just as much as he wants what is best for them. Trust him. Test his promises, and find them true:

His divine power has given us everything we need for life and godliness through our knowledge of him who called us by his own glory and goodness. Through these he has given us his very great and precious promises, so that through

> them you may participate in the divine nature and escape
> the corruption in the world caused by evil desires. (2 Peter
> 1:3–4)

One thing I have repeated through the years to single women is "with privilege comes responsibility." When they are thinking (or saying, if they are honest), "How come she gets to have sexual fulfillment and I don't?" I remind them that "she" has made a lifetime commitment to her husband. Whatever happens to him will also happen to her. She has inextricably attached herself to another person and has made a commitment that one makes to none other. To want to have the pleasure of a sexual relationship without a no-back-door commitment to a person is selfish and irresponsible.

As a single, you need to know that those who are married, even disciples, have to work at their relationship for it to be fulfilling and encouraging. They also have to work at their sexual relationship for it to be fulfilling and encouraging: he may want to be together more often than she does; she may feel resentment toward him in some other area and therefore, finds it harder to want to be with him sexually.

Every relationship needs constant maintenance. Don't believe Satan's lie that the sexual relationship in marriage is always an out-of-this-world experience day-in and day-out. It is exciting, encouraging and very special...but only if the couple continues to be selfless and giving to each other in other areas also.

Dealing with Temptation

As I stated earlier, you are a sexual being. You have hormones and you have the God-given ability to respond to sexual stimuli, both visual and physical. You are a woman, but you are a woman who is committed to sexual purity. How do you keep those two at peace with each other?

Temptation Is Not Sin

Jesus himself was tempted in every way that we are:

> For we do not have a high priest who is unable to sympathize with our weaknesses, but we have one who has been tempted in every way, just as we are—yet was without sin. (Hebrews 4:15)

Jesus was sexually tempted. He was a man, a real man. Not only that, he was a real *single* man. And he was tempted in every way that we are. The amazing thing is that he never once gave in to temptation—sexual or otherwise.

Temptation is not sin. Neither involuntary bodily responses nor specific temptations make us impure—only allowing either to drag us into sin. Consider the following passage:

> When tempted, no one should say, "God is tempting me." For God cannot be tempted by evil, nor does he tempt anyone; but each one is tempted when, by his own evil desire, he is dragged away and enticed. Then, after desire has conceived, it gives birth to sin; and sin, when it is full-grown, gives birth to death. (James 1:13–15)

When a sexual thought comes to us (maybe even a very bizarre one), we have a decision to make: "Will I go with it or not?" As disciples of Jesus, we have the power to say "No!" Our old nature (evil desire) drags us away and entices us to unite with it. But we can say "No!" We can say, "I will not unite with you." And we can simply get up and walk away.

On the other hand, when our old nature (evil desire) drags us away and entices us to unite with it, we can choose to give in. And when we do, the passage says that this union causes sin to be conceived. And when sin grows up, it gives birth to spiritual death. That is, our hearts become hardened; we no longer repent; and we are separated from God.

To understand the meaning of this passage, consider the following comparison: If a man who was not our husband wooed us and enticed us to have intercourse with him, we would say "No!" We would walk away. No union would occur. No child would be conceived. The concept is the same spiritually speaking. We have the power to say NO and walk away from any temptation—no union occurs and no sin is conceived:

> No temptation has seized you except what is common to man. And God is faithful; he will not let you be tempted beyond what you can bear. But when you are tempted, he will also provide a way out so that you can stand up under it. (1 Corinthians 10:13)

Just because you have a sexual response to stimulus does not mean that you have sinned. If pressure or stimulation of any type is brought to bear upon the vaginal area, you will often feel a response: lubrication and/or sensation that is the beginning of the build-up to orgasm. Orgasm is brought on by stimulation of the clitoris, which is "hidden" in the vaginal folds of the vulva. You will notice that during certain times of the month a sexual response comes more easily and quickly. That is because God's design generally ties this response to the time of ovulation—the time you can get pregnant. It makes sense, doesn't it, since one of the purposes of the sexual relationship is procreation?

So, when it takes very little stimulation for you to feel a "sexual stirring" in that area, just be on notice that you need to be careful. If you are dating or engaged, be on guard especially during that time to keep from stepping over the line from affection to passion—a very quick step!

On the other hand, if you are doing nothing to encourage or prolong this response, you have no reason to feel guilty. Remember to tell yourself, "I am a woman. I understand what is happening to my body. But the timing is not right for me to be sexually active in any way. In fact, it is sinful for me to be. So, I choose to keep my mind on pure thoughts and not to indulge myself by self-stimulation. It will leave me unfulfilled in the long run and is not God's perfect plan for me or my sexuality."

Why So Open?

You may wonder why I am being so explicit in my description of temptation. You may say, "You are causing me to struggle. I was sitting here, minding my own business, being pure, and you bring up all this stuff that is now giving me problems. I am even having the very experience that you described."

Please don't be frustrated with me. I am concerned that we are not talking enough about these things, and as a result, faithful women are feeling frustrated, confused and guilty. I would rather that you have a little extra struggle for five minutes or so, in order to have an understanding that will help you for however many years you are single. Many single women get so "guilted out" that they just give up on the whole pursuit of purity, giving in to whatever their sinful nature desires. I do not want that to happen to any of you.

Certainly, it is wrong to seek sexual stimuli. If you rent movies in order to see sexual scenes, if you listen to music with sexually explicit lyrics, if you read books or magazines with vivid sexual descriptions, if you try to see how close you can get to impurity without getting burned by it...you are giving up the protection that God wants to give you. You *should* feel guilty because you are not committing yourself to the purity that God calls his daughters to have.

Remember that "you are not your own; you were bought at a price. Therefore honor God with your body" (1 Corinthians 6:19–20).

If you do sin sexually in some way—thought or act—confess it quickly to God and to a sister. Then gratefully accept forgiveness without doing penance, and make a specific plan to avoid that sin in the future.

Sexual Dreams

We have all, married and single, had random, maybe even bizarre, sexual dreams. How often have you had a dream like that and awakened feeling ashamed, dirty, guilty? Our subconscious is not something we can program or control.

We live in a sinful, fallen, sex-crazed world, and stimuli are bombarding us every day. When we are asleep, all of the visual, emotional, spiritual input from our life is pulled together to make plots and scenarios that would vie for best screenplays at the Academy Awards.

My way of dealing with a sexual dream is to say, "Wow. That was random. That was weird. Where on earth did that come from? I sure don't want any part of that." And I decide just to move on with my day. Usually, after maybe a few times of the memory coming back to me, it goes away.

If you have a recurrent dream or if you just can't seem to get the dream out of your mind, talk with someone about it. Bringing in the light of revelation helps to dispel lingering thoughts and fears. In fact, many singles prefer to mention the dream to someone just to protect them from dwelling on it or being tyrannized by it.

Check to make sure that you are not focusing during the day on anything of a sinful, sexual nature. If you are not, then simply pray that God will help you to get proper perspective; do not let Satan bog you down with false guilt; set your mind on other things; and continue to do God's will.

Use Your Imagination for God

God has given us the gift of imagination. Satan, as usual, wants to use this gift for evil instead of for good. God tells us to imagine all that he can do in our lives and to pray about those exciting, encouraging and noble possibilities (Ephesians 3:20). Satan tells us to use our imaginations to indulge ourselves, to go anywhere we want to go, to ignore the boundaries that God has set for our mind pictures. His goal is to plunge us into the depravity described by Paul in Romans chapter 1...and to separate us from our Father forever.

So, when you are tempted with sexual, lustful thoughts, decide to use your imagination for good things. Take captive those thoughts that are setting themselves up against the knowledge of God (2 Corinthians 10:5) by replacing them with faithful spiritual imaginings. For example, if you see a good-looking guy and your mind begins to move in a sexual direction, using him in your imagination...immediately start thinking about him standing in the water being asked by your ministry leader, "Do you believe that Jesus is the Son of God?" Then imagine him going under the water and coming up, smiling and happy to have his sins forgiven. Pray for him, share your faith with him if possible, and then go about your business.

Married Friends

Sometimes people who love us and want us to be married are the very ones who make comments that hurt us and tempt us with discontentment and despair. One single sister told me that sometimes she is content with where she is in life, and then other times she is tempted with deep discontentment. She realized that there was a correlation between her feelings of discontentment and the comments of her married friends: "I don't understand why you aren't married yet. What is wrong with the brothers?" Statements like these do not help. First, you are tempted to think, "What is wrong with me?" Then you move on to being critical and thinking, "What is wrong with the brothers?" Neither thought is encouraging, and neither sets you up for trusting God's will for your life.

Be open with married friends. Let them know what encourages you and what doesn't encourage you. Probably the best things they can do are

1. Pray for you;
2. Set you up with dates;
3. Remind you that being faithful is more important in the eternal scope of things than being married.

It is my prayer that you have come to several strong convictions while reading this article:

- You are created by God to be a sexual being, and this is good.
- It is God's will for you to be celibate until you marry.
- God will help you to be pure, and will give you a full,

meaningful and exciting life as a single disciple.

- No thing or no one is worth giving away your salvation for.

Enjoy God. Enjoy life. Enjoy being a disciple. Enjoy being a woman...God's woman.

Whether you remain single or get married, live your life at the foot of the cross. Remind yourself every day that to lose your life is to find your life. This is the only truth that gives meaning and eternal security to anyone's life...married or single. And to God be the glory!

1. Sheila Jones, ed. *Life and Godliness for Everywoman, Volume 1* (Spring Hill, TN: DPI, 2001).

Building Up Your Husband
Life and Godliness for Everywoman, Volume One

A wife of noble character is her husband's crown,
but a disgraceful wife is like decay in his bones.

Proverbs 12:4

I talked with a friend of mine whose husband is not a disciple. I love her heart and her desire to build up her husband. She shared the above scripture with me and said, "I go after being a crown to my husband. I want to make him feel like a king." This of course does not mean that we want to become chambermaids for the king. It does mean that we want to

- show respect;
- be aware of and sensitive to his needs;
- do the things that make him feel loved;
- build him up instead of criticize him;
- be protective of him when he is vulnerable.

We are going to look at the lives of three women in the Bible and how they treated their husbands. We will meet

- a man who's up;
- a man who's down; and
- a man you don't want to be around.

Two of the wives did not build up their husbands, did not encourage them and did not make them feel like kings—(though, in fact, one of them really was a king!) One wife, however, did

178

show respect for her husband—a man who most would say did not deserve it.

The Wife of a Man Who Is Up (David)
Michal, wife of David and daughter of Saul (2 Samuel 6:12–23)

The Ark of the Covenant is being returned to Jerusalem. King David, wearing a linen ephod (priestly vest), is dancing "before the Lord with all his might." When his wife, Michal, sees him from her window, she despises him in her heart. David sacrifices offerings, blesses the people, gives them each a loaf of bread and a cake of raisins. Then he goes to his own home to bless it also. He comes in, so vulnerable, so childlike, so excited about the Ark of the Covenant being returned. His eyes are glistening, his adrenaline is pumping, his mood is expectant…and his wife, of all people, pours a figurative bucket of ice water all over him and his excitement and his joy.

Michal's response to David

- emasculated her husband;
- disrespected him;
- put him down;
- attacked him when he was most vulnerable;
- belittled him;
- ate away at his confidence.

As a wife today, you do the same thing when you

- are dissatisfied with how your husband provides for you;

- constantly criticize his judgment, his leadership, his habits;
- are negative and complaining;
- compare him to other men;
- do not support him in the things that mean the most to him;
- communicate that you do not desire him as a man (sexually).

Your husband needs your comfort and your support, not a critique of his performance. You might say to him, "You need to share your feelings with me more." When he tries, do you interrupt, disagree and finish his sentences? If so, he will decide, "Why try?" You need to support him in his strengths. Give positive reinforcement. Yes, be honest, but keep in perspective his good points as you are honest about what he needs to change. Mention the needed changes in the context of the good he already does. He should look forward to coming home because it is a place of affirmation. He shouldn't get more affirmation at work or from others. You should be his greatest fan!

The Wife of a Man Who Is Down (Job)
Job's wife (Job 1:1–22, 2:1–10)

God allows Satan to destroy everything that is meaningful to Job—his livestock, his servants, his livelihood, his children, and his health. In great grief and misery he looks to his wife to encourage him to remain strong. He is as down as anyone can get. Certainly his wife is in grief too...her ten children had all been crushed to death at one time. Job tries to maintain his faith and his spiritual integrity. But his wife is no help:

> His wife said to him, "Are you still holding on to your integrity? Curse God and die!"
> He replied, "You are talking like a foolish woman. Shall we accept good from God, and not trouble?"
> In all this, Job did not sin in what he said. (Job 2:9–10)

At a very vulnerable point, the point at which his faith was threatened more than it ever had been, he needed a wife who would hold on to faith herself. Why might his wife have responded this way? Maybe she was

- angry with God for what had happened;
- resentful that Job was still being faithful and she was not;
- feeling justified in cursing God herself;
- concerned that her social prominence and standing had been lost;
- feeling a loss of meaning in life because her children had died.

Sometimes a husband might be depressed because

- things are not going well at work;
- he does not feel respected by the children;
- life (and promotions) seem to be passing him by;
- he feels inadequate for the task before him;
- he is getting older and losing his hair;
- he has a disease or physical challenge.

Might you respond negatively? Might you

- secretly wish he were stronger and resent him for his weakness;
- tell him to just get over it;
- say "Now you know how I have felt through the years";
- feel cheated that his depression, disease or physical challenge limits or inconveniences you;
- complain about bad circumstances that triggered the depression?

Job needed a wife whose own faith was strong and not dependent upon his. He had obviously been a steady spiritual leader in the family through the years, and was continuing to be, even in very trying circumstances. It is possible that she had relied on his faith to maintain her own. When testing came her way, she saw the weakness of her own faith. She could easily have become a millstone around the neck of a man tumbling into the depths of faithlessness (if Job would have allowed it). Or she could have become a woman who trusted deeply in God as her deliverer and her comforter so she could have strength to share with a husband in much physical and emotional pain.

When your husband is down, more than anything he needs you to believe in him—even if at the moment he does not even believe in himself. He needs to know that you love him—even if he is not at the top of his game. And he needs to hear from your *mouth* that you believe in him and love him—not just from your actions.

The Wife of a Man You Don't Want to Be Around (Nabal)
Abigail, wife of Nabal (1 Samuel 25)

David sends servants to Nabal during the time of feasting and shearing his sheep. He and his men had not only treated Nabal's men kindly, but they had also protected them while they were in the fields with the sheep. David asks for whatever gift Nabal would send him. Nabal very unwisely mocks and shows great disrespect for David, and spurns his request. David is on his way to destroy all the males in Nabal's household when Abigail, Nabal's wife, intercepts him. In her actions Abigail showed strong spiritual qualities:

- great courage—She knew that David's aggression was aimed at anyone of Nabal's household who got in his way, but she rode quickly to meet David and his men.
- positive action—She could have whined and complained about Nabal's bad judgment, but instead she moved into action to do something positive.
- deep faith—She affirmed the faithfulness and goodness of God, and believed with all her heart that God's will would be done.
- generosity—She brought ample provisions for David and his men.
- honesty—She clearly evaluated and stated the situation, and she did not make excuses for her husband's actions. The next day she was honest with her husband about what had happened.

- love—She showed love for her husband by saving his livelihood and his life.
- sensitivity and self-control—It was not a good time to talk with Nabal when she returned since he was very drunk. So she waited until the next day when he would be more likely to listen and able to understand what had happened.

Hopefully your husband is not consistently "mean and surly" and lacking in judgment, but there are likely times he is easily irritated and makes bad decisions. He is human, just as you are. How do you respond? Negative responses would include the following:

- flying off the handle and making "You always…" statements
- whining and complaining when he makes decisions you don't like
- being an enabler and not being honest with him and others about the effect of his moods and judgments. This is certainly true if he is abusive in any way.
- giving up on God's view of marriage
- withdrawing your love until he is in a good mood or makes a decision you agree with
- asking him questions or talking "at" him when he is obviously focused on something else
- deciding that it is all your responsibility to make things go the way you think they should go

Positive responses would be the opposite of all the above:

- being self-controlled and keeping the perspective of his good qualities
- being proactive to help the decision work out and being willing not to say "I told you so" if it does not work out
- being honest with him (and with others) about the effect of his moods and his judgments on you (especially if he is abusive in any way), bringing light into the situation
- affirming God's view of marriage and doing your part to make it shine
- offering unconditional love
- waiting until opportune times to talk about potentially sensitive or explosive issues
- trusting God to take care of situations that you have no control over

Abigail was a courageous, resourceful, faithful woman. As she went to be David's bride, she was willing to be flexible and to accept the life he had to offer her. She had been accustomed to a life of relative luxury (notice the five attendants she had with her as she left to meet David). But David lived a nomadic life, with two wives in tow. Abigail did not vacillate or hesitate, but she followed her man, ready to support him and to trust her God.

Make a Decision

Each of us as wives has to decide whether we will be willing and ready to support and love our husbands no matter what life may bring. We will all be tested in this (as will our husbands). But loyalty brings intimacy. Love begets gentleness. Trust lays a foundation of peace. Let us be the wives God calls us to be, and let us each love the husband he has given us.

---

1. Sheila Jones, ed. *Life and Godliness for Everywoman, Volume 1* (Spring Hill, TN: DPI, 2001).

Teaching Children to Respect
Life and Godliness for Everywoman, Volume One

"I want to get *Wrestlemania*."

"No, Justin," said his mom. "We're going to get a video that is for you and your sister."

"But I want *Wrestlemania*. I want *Wrestlemania*."

"Justin, I don't want you to get *Wrestlemania*."

"But I'll pay you for it later."

"Justin, it's not the money. It's just that I don't want you to get it. It's not all that good. And anyway, your sister shouldn't see it."

"But I want it. She doesn't have to watch it with me. I'll watch it earlier."

"Justin, I'm not going to say No again!"

"But Mom, I want…"

On and on it went in the video store, with Justin becoming louder and louder and Mom becoming more and more frustrated.

Finally, it culminated: "Justin, you make me so mad. You always think you're going to get what you want. And you always do!"

That day Justin walked out of the video store tightly clutching his beloved *Wrestlemania*. He had gotten what he wanted, but he had lost what he needed—a mom who taught and expected respect from her child. Ten years from now the stakes will be much higher. Instead of watching *Wrestlemania*,

Justin will be driving the car when he wants to and coming home when he feels like it after doing whatever he wants to do. It won't really matter what Mom says because she will have trained him that he always gets his way. She will throw up her hands and helplessly lament, "Teenagers!" as if an incurable disease had befallen her child.

What can we, as disciples, do to teach our children to respect authority in their lives? How can we withstand the onslaught of strong-willed children who are determined to have their own way? How can we teach respect in a society that no longer demands or even expects it from their children?

Build the Proper Foundation (Matthew 7:24–27)

Jesus tells us to be wise builders and to build on his word:

1. Respect for God (Isaiah 5:12; Malachi 1:6)
2. Respect for husbands (Esther 1:20; Ephesians 5:33)
3. Respect for wives (1 Peter 3:7)
4. Respect for parents (Leviticus 19:3; 1 Timothy 3:4)
5. Respect for the aged (Leviticus 19:32)
6. Respect for leaders in the church (Hebrews 13:17)
7. Respect for those in authority (Romans 13:7)
8. Respect for other people (Ephesians 5:21)
9. Respect for leaders of the land (1 Peter 2:17)

As mothers, we

- must have a deep respect for God and for his word;

- cannot ask of our children what we ourselves are unwilling to give;
- should realize that we show disrespect for God if we do not expect our children to respect us;
- must disciple the heart, not just demand fearful obedience;
- should live a life that calls for respect.

Are You Showing Respect?

Look again at the list of people to whom you are to show respect. As you read through, ask yourself in each applicable area, "How am I doing in showing respect in this area?"

Do I jump headlong into my busy day without reading God's word or without praying?

Do I talk with friends at the beginning of a Sunday morning service when the Scriptures are being read?

Do I complain to the children about what a messy person their dad is or how frustrated I am with him?

Do I remember to call my parents often and involve them in the life of my family?

Do I usually think I have a better idea than my boss or supervisor?

Do I bad-mouth the leader of my country?

Do I yell at other drivers or complain about them under my breath?

Do I respond rudely when a sales clerk is not helpful?

Do I complain about a teacher when I don't understand what she is doing?

Show Respect for Your Child

- by not jerking, yelling, pulling, swatting, demeaning or making idle threats (these actions exasperate your child—Ephesians 6:4);
- by telling him your expectations ahead of time in new situations. (If you take him in unprepared and uninstructed, you could be to blame when he misbehaves. When you set him up for success, you are showing him respect. If after preparing and explaining, he misbehaves, your reason for discipline is clear and the discipline is deserved.)

Expect Respect

So often kids are in control and their parents feel helpless—no matter how smart or successful they may be in other areas. They don't like it. They sometimes don't even like their children because of what their children are doing to them. And often they lash out at their children in anger, which causes them to feel guilty. Then they overindulge to appease their guilt, and the child tightens his or her control. The cycle chokes the life out of the parent and the joy out of the child. Do you ever see this cycle in your relationship with your child?

You must calmly, patiently, but firmly, expect respect. Those who do not expect respect will respond in one or more of the following negative ways:

- fume
- get frustrated
- get frantic
- lash out
- yell
- lament and complain about the lack of respect
- blame the stage their child is going through (Toddlers! Preteens! Teenagers!)
- blame their husband for the child's behavior
- resent input from others

It is difficult to truly enjoy a disrespectful child because he

- is consumed with controlling and getting his way;
- cannot let down enough to enjoy what he is given;
- feels compelled to find some reason to be dissatisfied;
- is insecure;
- is unhappy;
- feels burdened to have a whole world just waiting for him to control it.

Practical Helps

Recognize disrespect

1. saying NO
2. hitting adult in authority
3. hitting the air
4. stomping feet
5. slamming the door
6. giving defiant looks
7. rolling the eyes
8. murmuring under breath
9. using a sassy tone
10. using a condescending tone
11. talking back
12. ignoring
13. constantly interrupting
14. pushing
15. lying
16. biting

Register shock at disrespect—your face, your demeanor, your words should make it unmistakably clear that his response is not acceptable. Sometimes parents respond with a sweet-talking, namby-pamby reply that tries to gently talk them out of being disrespectful. Unless you expect respect and teach him how to show it, you will not have it. If you beg your child to obey, he will realize he is in control and will decide that he has a choice in the matter. (And guess which choice he will usually make.)

Realize the message of culture—In so many situations, the child is in control. In their disrespect, some children feel not only equal to adults, they feel very much superior to them, their parents included. Commercials and sitcoms do their part to demean the role of parents and to exalt the role of the child. In this computer age, this age of entitlement, children feel they are the parent of their parents. And they will continue to think that until they are proven wrong by loving but firm parents who respect God and who call their children to respect them.

If children feel superior to their parents and the parents do nothing to change that perception, the children will transfer that feeling of superiority to God. They will feel that they know better than God. They can direct their own lives better than God can. Is that not the pervasive feeling of our culture? The Bible calls this feeling many different things: disrespect, rebellion, arrogance, disobedience. These are sins that separate people from the God who made them and who knows how they are to function.

Why Parents Do Not Expect Respect

- **Lack of love**—You may be showing affection and meeting physical needs, but if you are not training your child in this area of utmost importance, you are not loving him as God would have you love him.
- **Laziness**—It takes a tremendous amount of energy to train a child in a godly way. Consistent discipline takes consistent energy. You must not allow laziness to rob your child of the consistent training he needs in order to learn respect for God.

  An added note about laziness: We as disciples can become lazy and not take seriously our responsibility to help each other with our children. Other people often see more clearly what is happening in our relationships with our children. They see more quickly when we as parents are being harsh or being manipulated by our children. We must overcome our laziness

and "speak the truth in love" to each other concerning the attitudes and behavior of both parents and children. As families
and as a church, we will not grow properly unless this kind of
interchange is happening on a regular basis in our relationships.

• **Fear**—Because your child means so much to you and is such
a part of you, you can easily fall prey to fear as you make
decisions about how to respond to him. The apostle John
reminds us, though, that "perfect love drives out fear" (1
John 4:18). As we decide to love God and to love our children, we will have greater courage and will not give in to our
fears.

Listed below are some of the fears that can wrongly motivate us as parents.

**1. Fear that our children will not like us if we expect
respect from them.** Much of our view of ourselves as people
is the reflection of our children's view of us. More than the gen-
erations before us, we want our kids to think we are "cool." We
want to dress in a way that pleases our preteens or teens. We
shouldn't be out of date, but being accepted by our children
has become too important to many of us.

We also know that if we rub our kids the wrong way, they
will get upset at us. As a preschooler, they may say, "I don't love
you." As a preteen, they may say, "So-and-so's mom doesn't
make her do that. I wish you weren't my mom. I wish I had her
mom." As a teen they may say, "I hate you. You are ruining my

life!" These things hurt. We want more than anything to be a good parent who does right things with our children, and we want them to like us for it. But just mark it down, if you really try to do what is right for your child in God's eyes, you will probably hear statements like the preceding ones at some time from your child. But the parent with true "agape" love is willing to suffer at the hands of their children *for the sake of their children.* They are willing to work their way through the painful, though false, guilt that begs, "You are hurting them. Do whatever it takes to make them happy."

It is gratifying, though, to go through these rough times, and then have your grown or close-to-grown child thank you for sticking to your guns. In family devotionals our three girls have shared about their gratitude for our dogged determination to do God's will even when they didn't like us for it. If we call our children to show respect for us and God and others, they will not always like us for it. But some day, we generally find they will love us more than ever for it.

We have to find our acceptance and security deep in the heart of our God. Otherwise, we will allow fear of rejection to keep us from taking righteous stands and setting our kids up for true success.

2. Fear that our children won't respond well, and we will feel foolish in front of others. Our tactic here is to play down their disrespectful behavior: "He's just a boy." "She's just inquisitive." "They didn't understand what they were supposed to do." If we have a pretty good idea that our child will throw a fit if we correct him for disrespectful behavior, we are wary of doing so. What will we do when the fit comes? How will we save face and seem to be in control (when we know we most assuredly are not in control)? So, we deceive ourselves into believing that the behavior is not really that bad. Meanwhile, bad goes to worse as our child cries out to be curbed, to be disciplined. The more he or she acts out, the less inclined we are to respond because we sense that our control is slipping more and more. Sound at all familiar? We must decide which is more important—protecting our pride or loving our child.

If other disciples observe our interactions with our children, they can help us draw the line that should have been drawn long before. They can help us have the courage to expect respect and not to worry about how we come across to others in the meanwhile.

3. Fear that we will damage their self-esteem if we curb their self-expression. The current trend toward teaching our children is to encourage "self-expression." Whether through "inventive spelling" or "it's right because that is what I meant to say," kids are getting the message that even with the English language, they are calling the shots. As they enter middle schools, teachers are finding students harder and harder to correct grammatically because they feel basically justified to write any way they want to. No one can really say whether it is right or wrong because "I have simply written what is right for me."

So raising children in a society that urges self-expression to the nth degree, we must take a stand as disciples of Jesus. We must certainly be sensitive to our children's feelings, but we must not take that sensitivity to an extreme. God did not hold back from telling us to curb any behavior that is sinful. He is more concerned about saving our souls than about giving free rein to our self-expression. And we should have the same concern for our children.

God is the one who gives us the greatest self-esteem possible. When we are right with him and accepted by him, that is all that matters in the long run. We must believe that ourselves, and we must teach it to our children. To do God's will is always right and will never be detrimental to our sense of true self worth.

4. Fear that we might be unfair. Life is not fair. When we are too concerned that everything we do and every decision we make is totally fair for everyone involved, we can end up in inertia. We will spend useless time second guessing ourselves while teaching our children that all those who are in authority in their lives will always bend over backwards to make sure that everything is fair for them. Then when a teacher chooses someone else to be the lead in the class play, they will feel or even shout, "Unfair!" When they are half-a-point away from a B- and the teacher gives them a C+, they will say, "Unfair."

Certainly out of our own Christian values we want to be just and equitable, but just because one child receives candy in the morning while visiting the bank does not mean that another child who was in school at the time deserves to get candy too. It does not mean that because one child is spending the night with someone that we must rack our brains to figure out who the other one can spend the night with (because she is feeling sad and left out). Sometimes one gets to do things; another time the other gets to.

Paul reminds us, "Does not the potter have the right to make out of the same lump of clay some pottery for noble purposes and some for common use?" (Romans 9:21). There are times in life when others get to do something that we don't get to do. That's just the way it is—when you are six and when you are sixty. *But that's hard*, we think. Yes, it is. But it is also true. The Hebrew writer tells us to "endure hardship as discipline" (Hebrews 12:7). If we allow our children to have disrespectful and ungrateful attitudes because we are trying too hard to make life fair for them, we are out of bounds. We are encouraging the sense of entitlement that is rampant in our society today.

❄

Back to Justin and the video store (by the way, this interchange is one that I personally observed). I feel for that mom who felt absolutely helpless in an emotional duel with her child. I can remember times when I felt some of that same helplessness. There are no "how-to's" that are specific enough to cover all the parenting bases. There are no examples that will match up to your every life situation. There are no perfect role models as parents, except the Father himself. That's why faith and reliance upon God is the only way we can be parents who show respect ourselves and who expect and receive respect from our children.

Remember though, children are learning, just like we are. Each child will make many wrong turns on the road to adulthood, and so will you—on their road to adulthood. So be kind and patient with them. But also remember it is always right to expect what God expects and to train and discipline in love to bring about his expectations.

Sheila Jones, ed. *Life and Godliness for Everywoman, Volume 1* (Spring Hill, TN: DPI, 2001).